ONE BITE AT A TIME

ONE BITE AT A TIME

A True Story of Transformational Change and 7 Life Lessons Learned To Help You Live Your Best, Healthiest, Happiest, Most Inspired Life

Susan Van Hoosen

Copyright © 2016 Susan Van Hoosen
All rights reserved.

ISBN: 1539608522
ISBN 13: 9781539608523

For Sophia, who inspires me every day to do and *be* my best. Without your love, support and encouragement, this book would be just a dream without a deadline.

Contents

Introduction ································ix
Just as each chapter in our life is meant to teach us, each chapter in this book is a lesson learned to help and inspire you along your life's journey.

Chapter 1 Lesson: When Overwhelmed, Take It One Bite At A Time······························ 1
Chapter 2 Lesson: Making Tough Choices For The Right Reasons Always Works Out For The "Even Better"························· 35
Chapter 3 Lesson: How To Leverage Your Super Human Power. ···················· 61
Chapter 4 Lesson: Grief Lessons Learned ················ 68
Chapter 5 Lesson: Be Awakened By Animals ············ 125
Chapter 6 Lesson: Serving Others Serves Your Purpose···· 137
Chapter 7 Lesson: Embrace The Process ················ 145

Final Thoughts ························ 153
Acknowledgements ····················· 155
Inspirational Reading List ··············· 157
About the Author····················· 159

Introduction

As I AWOKE this Sunday morning, January 18, 2015, I lay in bed practicing my recent ritual of speaking gratitude out loud for having had a good night's sleep, for waking up feeling energized (which I've struggled with these past two years), for my warm bed, heat and electricity, my health, the sunshine, a good day yesterday, and my daughter Sophia, still asleep in her room.

Though I didn't know at that moment, this was the day I'd begin this book. I'd been thinking about writing a book for years, even before the consequential "shift" I've experienced. The theme of my story has changed and evolved, as my life has changed and evolved. It was as if I'd had to wait until the story and its lessons had unfolded. On this day, with a few promising hints from the Universe, I came to realize that I'd lived a transformational story that could help other people. We all have a story, and mine was getting lighter, brighter, and more meaningful, just like the feelings and signs I'd been receiving telling me that it was time to start writing my story.

I'd put a picture of a typewriter with a piece of paper titled *My Book* on my 2015 vision board to inspire me to get started. I'd become a deeper "seeker" in the last two years, yearning to know more about the other side, growing spiritually, becoming more awakened and closer to God, eager to feed my soul and serve my life's purpose. Earlier that week, I received a text message from Matt, my oldest "bonus" son, who was away at college. (I use the word *bonus* instead of *step* because my two boys are a bonus to my life.) His message read, "Found this and thought of you! 7 Steps to Master the Law of Attraction This Year," with a link to the web article of the seven steps. It was just what I needed that day. I was overwhelmed with love and gratitude for Matt and our connection.

That Sunday morning, as if a follow up to Matt's message, I received a plethora of amazing, hair-raising, goose-pimple-inducing signs and messages, starting with the daily inspirational calendar in my bathroom. The message on my calendar read, "If you aspire to be a published writer, Archangel Gabriel can help your dreams come true!" Wow! I smiled as I read this. I couldn't believe it and took it as an exciting nudge.

As was my morning routine, I went downstairs, started the coffee, let out and fed Rudy, our beloved pet Lab and one of the most loving spirits I've ever known, and walked downstairs to the basement to read my daily affirmation calendar *I Can Do It* by Louise Hay. Today's message read,

"I read books that enrich my soul and give me food for thought. There is always more to learn." Another goose-pimples moment for me. OK, I thought with a bigger smile, I get it! I've been reading more books for the sole purpose of enriching my spirit and learning more about writing my own book.

I've learned, usually the hard way, that sometimes it takes a brick to the head for us to finally get the message and learn life's lessons. And, as Oprah teaches, the lesson is repeated until it is learned. So what happened next was a tender brick—the one I needed to begin writing this book. I had just received a new deck of cards I'd ordered on Health and Wellness Affirmations that I had planned to use with my clients. I opened it for the first time because I felt drawn to it and was seeking and hoping to receive another message of reassurance (as if the first two weren't enough!). I asked Archangel Gabriel to guide me and the first card I picked read, "My Health Story and the Law of Attraction." Reading it sent chills down my body. What else did I need? I had a story to share and a deep desire to help others. I knew with everything in me all would be well, and I would start writing this book and embracing the process "one bite at a time."

I share these incidents with you so that you can be awakened to the messages, signs, and whispers, both within you and from the Universe, to help guide you along your own journey. The fact that you're reading this book indicates you too are seeking more meaning and purpose for your life, which is perhaps in a state of transformational growth.

My purpose and my hope is that this book will inspire others to live their best life, even and especially when they've been brought down to their knees by loss, illness, tragedy, or whatever challenge knocks them down. My hope is that my story helps serve as a tool for you along your own journey and, if needed, will help you reframe your story, recognizing yourself as the "victor" and not the victim of your life. I want you to rise up into the heroine or hero of your own life. May you find hope, enlightenment, faith, inspiration and awaken to the possibilities and dreams stirring within you. May this nudge you forward to where you are meant to be. If you too are grieving or suffering, may this help you in some way as you move *through* the grief and pain, and move toward your new normal. As one of my favorite wellness goddesses, Dr. Christiane Northrup, teaches, and I too now coach, "We gotta feel it to heal it!" May this book help you feel, create, and live your best, healthiest, happiest, most inspired life, *even and especially when* life knocks you down.

CHAPTER 1

Lesson: When Overwhelmed, Take It One Bite At A Time

> "How do you eat an elephant?
> One bite at a time."
>
> —Trent Van Hoosen

I was never a one-bite-at-a-time kind of girl. I don't think I was born or wired that way by nature. Instead, I had always prided myself in juggling, managing and accomplishing multiple tasks and projects all at once—a multitasking addict, if you will. My husband, however, was more of the laid-back, easy-going, mindful, slower-paced (what I used to think of as too slow, or not fast enough for me at times!), no worries, one-thing-at-a-time guy. I wished many times in the midst of my type-A self-imposed chaos that I could be more like him; more like him meant being more present, not stressing myself out over running behind or doing too many things at once, not reacting emotionally, and not worrying. He loved to tell me that he didn't need to worry because I did enough worrying for both of us. When we were faced with a significant challenge or an important life situation, he would say, "Babe, how do you eat an elephant? One bite at a time." During our marriage we were faced with quite a few tough life situations and often all at once. Business bankruptcy, job losses, deaths, blended family and ex-spouse dynamics, surgeries, and miscarriages, just to name a few. He almost always remained level headed and my steady, solid, peace-making, one-bite-at-a-time rock.

We had the rare kind of marriage my single friends said they wanted to have one day and many of my married friends said they wished they had. Years after we married, people would still comment that we were in the "honeymoon stage." I guess it was because we grew more madly and maturely in love and still felt and acted like we were dating. Yes, we were sometimes that couple who engaged in public displays of (respectful) affection; the couple that made others roll their eyes and say, "Get a room." We were consumed with our love and couldn't get enough of each other, mainly because we were so grateful for one another and we knew what we had was rare and special. We both had previously experienced unhealthy marriages and had worked on ourselves with counseling and on our own before we met, so we got the better version of each other, which we didn't take for granted and nurtured every day. Everything we did, we did with passion—we loved passionately, cooked and worked out together with passion, loved our children and blended family with passion, and even argued with passion. We didn't mind our intense disagreements because the making up part was also filled with passion.

There were two things Trent told me quite often. First, if he were to die tomorrow, I'd made him the happiest man alive. Secondly, no one would ever love me as much as he did. Another frequent thing he would say is that I saved his life. This one would later haunt me. He said all three of these things when we first met and fell in love and he told me all three the week he died. I believe his spirit knew what was coming.

A long weekend in Nashville, Tennessee, had been on our weekend-getaway bucket list for a while. We both loved country music and exploring new destinations together. So the Saturday after my oldest bonus son's playoff football game, we headed off to Nashville to celebrate our wedding anniversary and for a much needed getaway. Trent had been under pressure at his job and hadn't been feeling well. Although he didn't complain, the circumstances surrounding his job led me to complain about the way I felt he was being mistreated. Leading up to our trip, I'd asked him to see a doctor about the fatigue, chest pains and shortness of breath he'd been experiencing—clear signs that something was seriously wrong. As I look back and as I write this now, it's so obvious that these are clear signs of a multitude of fatal illnesses, yet neither of us could have ever imagined at the time just how serious it was. Trent was otherwise the epitome of health, strength, and fitness.

At six feet and three inches, he was built like a professional football player and had been doing CrossFit workouts for the last two and a half years. He had just turned forty-six three weeks prior and said he felt like he was in the best shape of his life, even more so than when he played college football at Iowa State. He said he was too busy with work and didn't feel he could get away for a doctor's visit, even though his job required him to be in a hospital working with doctors almost every day. I knew he felt his job was on the line and that he needed to work extra hard to prove himself. There were changes happening at his company and because he didn't fit the mold of the ego-driven culture he worked in, we were concerned.

As our weekend trip came closer, I finally told him that if he didn't make an appointment with the doctor, I would, and he knew me well enough to know I would. Two days before we left, he told me he had a conversation with a doctor-friend of ours he'd run into at the hospital that day. Based on what Trent had told him, our cardiologist friend said it could be a heart issue or lung cancer and that his office would schedule an appointment as soon as possible. Not the news I wanted to hear, but I was relieved he was finally going in for testing. I asked him if he'd told our doctor-friend about his blot clot surgery four years prior, thinking it had to be related. He had told him everything.

An excerpt from "Susan's Story," posted on my website www.inspiredbyfitness.net in February 2013:

The last weekend of October 2012, we spent a long weekend in Nashville, TN to celebrate our wedding anniversary. We loved country music and exploring new cities and locally-owned eateries together. On the mornings after fun late evenings at 'Country Music Row,' we still got up to work out at the hotel gym and did our best to have a healthy lifestyle balance on vacation.

*Three days after we returned home, Trent's heart stopped and he died unexpectedly from a blood clot that had traveled to his lung. He had just turned 46 three weeks prior and was excited about his work, his life and our family's future. As I write this, it still doesn't seem real even though I am **moving forward one day at a time as best as I can for the kids—Matt, Joe and Sophie, to honor his memory and my own life**. Although Trent was physically strong, fit and appeared to be very healthy, he had a pre-existing condition of DVT—Deep Vein Thrombosis, not only hereditary, but if ignored the blood clot can travel to the lung or heart and be fatal.*

That's the brief version I shared when I created my website for my new business, offering others my self-prescribed grief therapy. I don't even remember writing it or most of my blog posts, and I wasn't able or ready to share the details in writing until now. As you can imagine, there's much more to the story.

That last weekend, when we finally arrived at our hotel in Nashville after being delayed two hours by construction, we had already had some deep conversations and were ready to unwind. Although we always thrived on having deep, meaningful conversations together about life, death, past experiences and revelations, future hopes and dreams, we talked more about life and death this trip. Trent's health scare was weighing on the back of both of our minds but we were determined to let it go, have fun, and not worry. Surely it was something minor that just needed to be checked out. We'd overcome so much and were excited about all that was ahead for us and our family. We were greeted in our hotel room with chocolate covered strawberries and a bottle of champagne from our dear friend Dorothy who worked for the hotel chain and had helped secure our hotel room. Alongside the strawberries and champagne were a dozen long stemmed red roses from Trent with a "Happy Anniversary" card. We both felt we were the luckiest couple alive.

The Nashville trip was wonderful, but different from our usual getaways. Although we rose each morning to work out together, explored the streets and sights of Nashville with wonder, visited the Country Music Hall of Fame, reveled in the nightlife at downtown Music Row, we found ourselves calling it a night earlier than usual and resting more in between outings. I kept asking if he had heard from the doctor's office about his appointment, but he had not. When I suggested that we call and follow up, reiterating that we needed to take charge of our health, he firmly reassured me the doctor's office would call. When I say firmly, I don't mean in a gruff, harsh way. Trent wasn't the kind of person to make a fuss, voice a complaint, return bad food at a restaurant, or follow up with people who said they would take care of something when clearly the ball had been dropped. I, on the other hand, was this kind of person (and still am, but I handle these situations in a gentler, more open way now, thankfully) and told myself I was calling the doctor as soon as we got back.

Our last night we decided to have dinner at the hotel and stay in for the night, which was uncharacteristic of us, but Trent was tired and I knew he was feeling worse than he let on. We had also been out late the night before and probably had a few more drinks than we should have. How many times had we said, "We are never drinking that much again"? At dinner, we talked about our health and fitness and that the one thing getting in the way for us both in being our healthiest and fittest selves was drinking alcohol. We didn't consider ourselves hard core drinkers, but we did like to enjoy wine with dinner on an occasional Tuesday, Wednesday, Thursday, or Friday night and a couple of cocktails on the weekend or a couple of beers watching sports or after doing yard work. We knew many people who lived a similar lifestyle. Although we knew we didn't have an addiction problem with drinking, when we broke it down, we could acknowledge that drinking was a regular part of our lifestyle and that it wasn't worth the problems or headaches it caused. We made a commitment that night to step away from drinking and I hoped that it would help Trent feel better as well.

On the drive back home, I again asked if the doctor's office had called yet with his appointment time. There was no call yet. I was furious and scared at the same time. We arrived back home on Tuesday, later than expected and after the doctor's office had closed. I told myself I was going to call first thing in the morning. That night Sophia (just twelve years old) woke up vomiting her macaroni and cheese all over herself, her bed, and the floor in her bedroom. Trent got up, tired as he was, to help clean up, and I took Sophia downstairs to the basement to sleep. He brought a bucket to have beside her as she lay on the couch, vomiting almost every hour. She didn't stop throwing up until the next day. I've never been the kind of mom to rush to the doctor for every little thing, but after twelve hours of throwing up, I called the doctor. They said she needed to get it out and if it persisted to call back. Trent left for work and I stayed home with Sophia, still in the basement, as she could barely move and was still getting sick. Luckily, I had taken the whole week off for vacation and could stay home to care for her. Little did I know that I would not return to work for over two months. The only thing she'd eaten all day was saltine crackers, ginger ale, and sips of water to keep her hydrated. Finally, at 2:00 p.m., I called the doctor back and told them something wasn't right and that we needed to see a doctor. They told me to take her to the ER. I called Trent and said I was taking her to Saxony, the hospital he was working at that day. However, he said their ER wasn't equipped for this type of admission, so I took her to another hospital, where they admitted her and injected an IV to replenish fluids. While in the hospital room, I received a text from one of my best friends who lives in Cincinnati, Dee, which said, "Hi, Susan, just letting you know that I'm praying for you." I thought, *Wow*. I knew Dee was a soul sister kind of friend, and though we shared spiritual beliefs and conversations, we hadn't ever randomly texted one another in this way. She must have sensed something was going on at the time. Dee had lost her father six months prior. She was heartbroken and seeking connection to the other side and had shared the story of a white dove that was flying by her car along the highway one day after her father's passing, at a time when she was thinking about and missing him. We both knew that a white dove in Ohio is not a regular sighting and felt that was her father visiting her. I sent her a white dove Ty Baby stuffed animal shortly after. I got the significance and message, even then. But what would be revealed later from her text was a divine moment and a symbol of the Universe supporting us.

When Sophia and I finally left the hospital, it was close to five thirty on Halloween night. I called Trent on the way home, and he said he was tired and not feeling well. Exhausted myself, I told him to shut the blinds, turn off the porch light, go to bed, and forget about the trick-or-treaters. When we came home, Trent was lying on the couch next to the Halloween basket of candy. He had been getting up to greet the trick-or-treaters. I took Sophia and Trent up to bed, turned off all the lights, and tucked them both in. I don't remember the rest of the night.

The next day, Trent left for work, and Sophia stayed home recovering from the flu. I called the doctor on his mobile phone and left a voice mail letting him know no one had called Trent with an appointment time and that it was urgent that he get in before the weekend. He called me back in less than an hour and said that "heads were rolling because someone had dropped the ball in not calling Trent." I told him I was scared and that something was seriously wrong. He said he was concerned too and would get him in that day or the next, which was Friday. When Trent came home later after work, he told me he had an appointment the next day at noon. I smiled, as I knew he didn't know that I had called. He headed straight for the couch to lie down until it was time to go to the high-school football dinner held every Thursday before Friday's game for players and parents. Joe, a freshman in high school, had come over early to work out but Trent was too tired. I remember looking at Joe sitting at the breakfast bar, glancing over at his dad, napping on the couch, and saying to him, "He's really tired from a big week and not feeling one hundred percent, but he'll work out with you this weekend." We hadn't shared with the kids that Trent hadn't been feeling well and didn't want to burden them. I stayed home with Sophia, and Joe and Trent left for the dinner. I asked Trent to call me on the way home so I could have dinner ready for him, since he usually didn't eat at the pitch-in dinners.

On the way home from the dinner, Trent called and asked if he could just have some soup and if I would mind if he went to bed after. As we sat at the breakfast bar, eating soup, both exhausted in our own way, a pit started to grow in my stomach. I kept praying that he would be OK and was glad he would be going to the doctor the next day.

After I tucked him in, I came back downstairs to watch the Country Music Awards on TV. I kept praying that everything would be OK. When I checked on him later, he chuckled and asked if I came up for some booty time. We both laughed as we knew how funny and impossible this was the way he was feeling.

The next morning came early. Trent got out of bed and gasped in pain as his foot hit the floor. He said his leg hurt, and I begged him to stay home and just rest until the doctor's appointment at noon. He said he had to go to the 7:00 a.m. meeting at the hospital and that there was no one else who could go in his place. We went back and forth over him not going, but he was determined to go. As he rinsed off in the shower, I could see he was in pain. It would be Sophia's first day back to school after being sick. When she came downstairs to the kitchen, she heard us debating and me asking him to stay home. When she asked if everything was OK, we told her yes. She kissed him good-bye and headed off to school. As I walked him out to his rig, as he liked to refer to his car, I once again pleaded with him not to go and kissed him good-bye, for what would be our last kiss good-bye.

Physically and emotionally exhausted, I headed back up to bed to get some rest.

At 8:03 a.m., I heard the house alarm beep and Trent's footsteps downstairs and then up the stairs. I was so relieved he was back home. As his footsteps got closer, I sat up to greet him. He walked to the edge of the bed, looked deep into my eyes, and then collapsed to the floor. I sprang out of bed, screaming, trying to hold him up. I remember saying I was calling 911. When I got up to my phone, I saw that he had urinated. He was gasping for air, breathing heavily. I sat under him, trying to hold him up. Within minutes, the ambulance arrived. I ran downstairs to let the EMTs in and ran back up, crying hysterically, now that help had arrived. There were three of them including a woman named Kelly who was trying to calm me down. I told her what happened, while the two male EMTs were working on Trent. I watched in disbelief. I remember hearing him say he couldn't get to the bathroom. As they strapped him in a chair to get him downstairs, I remember being scared they couldn't hold him up, as they were smaller than he was. When they got him downstairs, I remember standing by the front door, as they held him in the chair to carry him out, looking at each other and telling him everything would be OK. In my shocked state of mind I was telling myself I needed to drive separately so I would have a car to bring him home in later. I didn't ride with him in the ambulance where he would take his last breath minutes later. By this time, my neighbor Jean had come in and was instructed by Kelly (the EMT) to not allow me to drive. My neighbor said she had to get her kids on the bus and would take me to the hospital. As soon as I got dressed, I ran out the door to get in my car; I wasn't waiting. As I tried to pull out of my driveway, still crying, she stepped behind my car and stopped me with her own body, then got me to move so she could drive. As we pulled out of my driveway, Carrie, one of my best friends, called me to check on how Sophia was doing. What I believe now to be a divine intervention call, for it would be Carrie who would carry me through the moments to come. I had called her when Sophia got sick that week. I was hysterical and told her what happened and asked her to call her ex-husband, who happened to be the doctor Trent had talked to and had the appointment with for noon that day. When we pulled into Saxony Hospital's ER entrance, Carrie was there waiting with a look on her face that made my heart pound even harder. She and my neighbor walked me in, holding me up. Carrie told someone that I needed to see Trent, and a doctor had us come into a room, first saying she needed to talk to me first. When I walked in, she said, "You know his heart stopped beating in the ambulance, right?" No, I didn't know that, and I couldn't process what it meant, so I said, "OK so what happens if you can't get it to start again?" Wow, when I write this I see how much in denial I was. Rationally, I know that when someone's heart stops beating, they will die, but I wasn't accepting that as an option. She looked at me stone cold in the eyes and said,

"Well, he'll die." I got up and said, "That is not going to happen." Carrie walked me into the next room where Trent lay, cut open, hooked up to machines, surrounded by five or six hospital workers, working on and around him. I handed Carrie my phone and told her to call for help. I wouldn't be able to look at my phone for three or four days later, unable to respond or function. For the next hour and a half, they worked on him, taking turns administering compressions, while I pleaded with them to keep trying, rubbing his feet, telling him to wake up so we could see Matt's football game. I was in complete shock and disbelief. Finally, one of the doctors stopped, looked at me, and said there was nothing more they could do. By this time, my parents, three of my friends, Jacqueline, Loretta, and Kathy, one of our Pastors, Pastor Joe, my boss Tracy, and another dear friend Patty whom I also worked with had shown up. As the hospital workers left the room and my family and friends came in, I spread my arms across Trent's bare chest, sobbing, refusing to leave. I'd asked Carrie to call the boys' mom, and she came to the hospital. We agreed she would go straight to the school to tell them, and let them decide if they wanted to see him at the hospital. When the time came to leave, Jacqueline drove me home in my car. She would continue to remain by my side throughout the following days, weeks and months to come. It wasn't how I'd pictured driving home from the hospital that day. I don't remember much, but I do remember her saying I would get through this and something about how strong

I was. I was visibly shaking, still hysterical, and in shock. My world has just come to a halt and erupted right in front of me. I didn't feel strong at all and I couldn't imagine how I would ever get through it. I just wanted to go with him. When we came back home, neighbors and cars had already started to arrive, filling our street and front yard. Carrie and her husband left to pick up Sophia from school and bring her home, where I would be faced with telling her the tragic news.

An excerpt from Sophia's journal:

> *How do you do it? How do you tell someone that their parent passed away, when they already had a gut feeling that they did. I was in the middle of fourth period with my friends and we were laughing away when I heard these sirens, for some reason I just had this weird feeling that it was my bonus dad (Who I called Big Daddy because when we first met when I was 5 he was so tall and big and would let me hang on him like a monkey). Then suddenly my teacher's phone rang. At that moment I knew in my gut something was not right. My teacher told me I had to go down to the front office. My whole body felt this numbness inside me. As I was walking down the steps, I remember saying under my breath "please don't be Big Daddy, please don't be Big Daddy." I walked up to the lady at the front desk asking what was wrong. She had told me it was a family emergency and someone was on their way to get me. I then asked her if*

it was my dad and she said she couldn't tell me…ARE YOU SERIOUS! I WANTED TO SCREAM AT HER! Right then I knew it was him, only I was shouting in my head, please be someone else. How cruel though? Here I was wishing someone else to be dead. I realize now I wouldn't wish this pain on anyone. Fourth period had passed and let me tell you I was a starving 12 year old. It had felt like I was waiting forever. Finally I saw someone walking in, hoping it was my mom, only to have it be her friend Carrie and her husband. We got in the car and I immediately asked if it was Big Daddy. She said that my mom will talk to me when I get home. When we pulled on to my street there were what seemed like a billion cars lined up on the side of the road. I knew that wasn't a good sign. It was like I knew what to expect. When I tried to get out of the car they tried to stop me and make me wait but I threw the car door open and ran as fast as I could to my house, only to stop at the front steps to see my grandma sitting in the chair in my living room with her head down. I walked in and when everyone saw me they began to stop talking. There was not a word spoken. I turned into the kitchen to find my mom sobbing. I asked her what was wrong and she said "Um…Sophia so sorry, Big Daddy passed away this morning. I dropped to the floor and burst into tears as my mom joined me saying "I know, I know, I'm so sorry. By then, everybody in the house was crying even more. I knew I couldn't be around it so I went outside with my dog Rudy. When I got to the curb I could see this car speeding down to where

I was. In it was screaming helpless boys...my brothers. They got out of the car and threw themselves on me bursting into tears. It was one of the saddest moments that I had experienced of my life. Here I was, a twelve year old girl that was going through the unfathomable...So here is my question. How does one tell somebody that their parent passed away? There shouldn't be an answer to this. Absolutely nobody should have to go through this. But we did.

The only thing I remember about telling her was her immediate question before she broke down into tears, "What about the boys?" she asked. I knew she feared that losing Trent meant we could lose the boys and our family. What I would later learn to do to help her through is what Brene' Brown teaches us in her Parent Manifesto shared in her book, *Daring Greatly*.

What transpired the rest of that day and the days to follow is blurry, yet there are moments that are so clear. Shortly after Sophia got home, Matt and Joe arrived. I knew they were there before they walked through the door as I heard a loud bang and knew without seeing it that Matt had punched the wall in the garage on the way in. When they walked in, he grabbed me to hold on tightly as we both just wept. I remember seeing Joe silent, sitting on the kitchen bench, struggling to hold himself up, tears in his eyes, confusion on his face.

The house was filled with people the entire day and night. People kept coming and showing up for us. That night was the high school football sectional playoff game where Matt, a senior, was to play as part of the starting lineup.

November 8, 2012

An article that appeared on the front page of the *Indianapolis Star*:

FISHERS, Ind.—It was four days after Matt Van Hoosen had been pulled out of his fourth-period German class and the rest of his life started. Four days? It seems like four months. Sitting in a chair at his kitchen table, Matt is at ease talking about what is next for him, his family, his younger brother. Then, that smile. A smile so wide and bright it illuminates even the dark corners of the kitchen. It comes when he recalls the CrossFit workouts his dad put Matt and his friends through to prepare for football season. Trent Van Hoosen did them too, carving out a makeshift gym in his garage for pull-ups, push-ups, squats and other exercises.

"He's 46 and he's out there doing the same workouts I am," Matt said with a laugh at the memory. "That's awesome. That was one of his passions."

In that moment, Matt looks just like his dad, or what his dad must have looked like at 17. People always commented on how much Matt reminded them of his dad. Their smiles. Their can-do attitude. Their physical and mental strength.

Trent Van Hoosen died last Friday, a victim of a blood clot in his chest. The devastating news spread through Fishers High School like a brush fire, shaking a school, a community and a football team to its core.

Matt and his dad always had football. Matt is a senior, a starting outside linebacker. After every home game, Trent, a former Iowa State offensive lineman, would wait along the chain link fence at the gate. Two weeks ago, after Fishers defeated in-town rival Hamilton Southeastern 42–7 in the sectional semifinal, father and son shared a long embrace.

"He had tears in his eyes," Matt said.

It was the last time Trent saw Matt play.

Hugging and crying
Matt was in a fog in the hours after receiving the news. When he arrived at his stepmother Susan's house that afternoon with his younger brother, Joe, a freshman at Fishers, there were already a couple dozen people there. Two of his closest friends, senior linebackers Liam Duddy and Robbie Peck, arrived later that afternoon, as did Fishers coach Rick Wimmer and Matt's position coach, Pat Schooley.

"A lot of hugging and crying," Duddy said.

Nobody talked about football. Fishers was hosting McCutcheon that night in the sectional championship, though it wasn't expected to be much of a game. Fishers defeated McCutcheon 34–6 during the regular season.

Matt didn't plan to go.

"I wasn't really ready for that," he said. "But the closer it got to game time, I felt like I needed to be there."

So Matt went, dressed in street clothes. He left his No. 49 jersey and game pants at home. Wimmer spoke with him briefly before the game, telling Matt he was glad to have him there. His teammates did the same.

Then the game started. It was awkward, for Matt and the team.

"It was definitely a different mood than there usually is on game day," Peck said. "That mood carried over to the game."

Fishers trailed 6–3 at halftime. The season, filled with so much promise after the win over HSE the week before, was teetering on the edge.

The locker room was glum at halftime. Tony Farrell, the defensive backs coach, approached Matt and asked him if he wanted to play.

"I thought he was joking," Matt said. "I said, 'Can I?'"

Just hours after losing his father, his biggest fan, Matt was headed back to the field to play for him. He pulled on a No. 49 freshman jersey and a pair of medium pants that were too tight, and jogged out to the field a couple minutes into the third quarter. The crowd quickly realized what was happening and chanted Matt's name.

"You couldn't't have written a more dramatic scene," assistant coach Curt Trout said. "When he ran out on to the field to a standing ovation, it was so emotional and awesome all at the same time."

Two plays after Matt entered the game, he sniffed out a screen pass and belted the running back. He paused, and then looked up and pointed to the sky.

"I didn't plan on that, I just felt it," said Matt as Fishers would score 35 consecutive points to advance to Friday's regional championship with a 38–13 victory. "During the game, I was talking with (my dad) a lot. I felt like he was there with me. I know for a fact he wanted me to be out there. That's what he would have wanted me to do."

You couldn't forget him
A day later and nearly 1,000 miles away, in Grand Forks, N.D., Chris Mussman was preparing his North Dakota football team for its final home game of the season. He hadn't heard about Trent Van Hoosen's death until he received a text message from former teammate Gene Williams minutes before kickoff.

He quickly called Williams back to confirm.

"I didn't handle it well," said Mussman, who roomed with Van Hoosen for away games at Iowa State in the late 1980s. "I was sort of standing there in a fog and one of our assistant coaches asked me what was wrong. I told him I'd lost a friend and teammate. It sort of permeated through our team. After the game (a 33–29 North Dakota win), a number of players told me they wanted to win this one for me and my friend.

"That was very special."

Trent Van Hoosen came to Iowa State as a walk-on out of Iowa's Newton High School in 1985. He was a linebacker, but was quickly moved to offensive guard and earned a scholarship. He started for three seasons and was part of a team that went 6–5 under Jim Walden in 1989, just one of two winning seasons for the program from 1981–99.

Van Hoosen started alongside future NFL players Williams and Keith Sims on the offensive line.

"That was probably the best offensive line we've had in the last quarter century," said Tom Kroeschell, an associate athletic director at the school. "(Trent) came back for a reunion a few years ago and said, 'You don't remember me do you?' I said, 'Of course. No. 54.' You couldn't forget him."

Van Hoosen is **easy to spot on old YouTube clips**. After touchdowns or big gains, No. 54 was almost always the most jubilant player on the field.

"There were some years in there where we weren't very good," said Tim Murphy, a former student trainer at Iowa State. "But Trent always made it fun. And he knew all of the trainers' names, which was not stereotypical for a football player."

Williams was talented, but didn't love football like Van Hoosen. There were even times he thought about giving it up altogether in college.

"I'm not going to tell you I was 'rah, rah' football," said Williams, who went on to play nine years with the Miami Dolphins, Cleveland Browns and Atlanta Falcons. "I liked the games, but hated the parts that led up to it. But 'Horse'—I always called him that—kept me going. He'd always say, 'You've got nothing better to do on Saturdays than play football.'"

Mussman had reconnected with Trent in the past six months as Matt considered pursuing football in college. Mussman appreciated those recent conversations with Van Hoosen.

"He was the type of person you wanted to be around," Mussman said. "He had a way of making you feel good about yourself when you were around him. That's a special quality to have."

Love notes

For Trent's 45th birthday last October, Susan, Matt, Joe and his stepdaugther Sophia presented him with a wooden box. Inside were written notes,

45 from Susan and 15 apiece from the three kids, with things they loved about Trent.

Some were funny. Joe wrote, "I love your dancing," and Matt, "I love how all my friends think you are huge."

Others, in retrospect, are heartbreaking. From Joe: "I love it how you still play football in the backyard with me," and "I love how you, me and Matt have late night pizza nights." From Matt: "I love how you push me to set goals for myself and we talk about them often," and "I love I can talk to you about anything."

It is comforting to Matt that he and his brother and sister had a close relationship with their father. He's thought about that a lot in these long days since Friday, especially at Monday's service when he was surrounded by his Fishers teammates—dressed in their jerseys—and hundreds of other people his dad had known.

"He treated everybody with respect," said Eric Hohlt, who coached youth football with Trent, "whether he'd known you for 20 years or 20 minutes."

Matt is setting goals. New goals. He wants to stay close to home for college so he can attend Joe's games, like his dad did for them both. He wants to be there for Joe, waiting at the end of the chain-link fence when he comes off the field. After the football season, he wants to train for the CrossFit Games and compete in his dad's honor.

And Friday night? Well, tonight Matt wants to make his father proud. His Fishers teammates will wear "TV" and "49" helmet stickers to honor the Van Hoosen family for the regional game against Fort Wayne Snider.

His dad won't be there, waiting for him by the locker room. But he will be with him out there on the field, in his heart and in his mind. Watching and smiling with that big grin.

"I hope that I can have the same presence he had," Matt said. "I guess I'd call it charm. He had that. I hope I can carry it on."

As it became late in the evening and most people had left, Jacqueline told me that Carrie and Kathy were going to stay with me that night and that she and Loretta would be staying the next night. I realized then that I was on watch and they were worried about what I might do, afraid to leave me alone. I didn't sleep that night until the early morning hours. Sophia lay next to me asleep all night. When I opened my eyes the next morning and turned to see Sophia and not Trent, it became real, and I had to face waking up to the fact that Trent was not there and had really died. I immediately began sobbing and didn't stop for hours. Carrie's mom, Billie, who has been my longtime friend and mentor, came to comfort me how a mom would. My own mom, who suffered from Parkinson's disease, was in shock and unable to help me for she was grieving too, realizing this day was the fiftieth anniversary of her mother's death.

I believe God gives us really great girlfriends in place of sisters, whom I never had, but I've always been blessed with the best girlfriends. It is my girlfriends who swept in, took charge, and saved me and carried me through that day and the days and months to come. They showed up, not asking what they could do, but seeing and doing what needed to be done. I remember my friend Carla doing laundry and cleaning the kitchen and my friend Cheryl bringing and placing multiple boxes of tissues around the house. I vaguely recall being puzzled by someone else doing our laundry and the multiple boxes of tissue, to soon see that the tissue boxes would quickly be emptied and that I wouldn't have the energy to do laundry. It's the little things that make a difference. If we're lucky enough, we get to have friends who not only give us different things we need but that we can give of ourselves for what they need. I am blessed to have a diverse group of really great girlfriends who each have her own unique gifts, talents, quirks, and qualities I love. I've found when you're a strong woman, you attract and are attracted to strong female friendships. Most of my friends are really strong women with big personalities and super-charged lives. Each of them showed up to save and carry me through in her own special way, showing me I wasn't alone.

That Sunday, Dorothy, one of my dearest friends, flew in from California. She's the one who had helped set us up in the hotel in Nashville. She loved Trent and he loved her. We had built many memories together over the years. I was blown away when she arrived from across the country. The next day my friend Dee (who texted me when I was at the ER with Sophia two days before Trent passed) showed up from Ohio. I was in my bathroom trying to pull myself together and get ready for Trent's Celebration of Life Service, when Dee stormed up into my room, visibly shaken. The only thing I remember is her saying, "You know why I texted you on Wednesday?" I said, "Because Sophia was in the hospital?" She said, "No, because I was reading the book *Heaven Is For Real* and God told me to pray for you." I knew then with everything in me that God was preparing me and those close to me for what was to come.

I would later learn from Jacqueline that another friend, who has a gift of reading palms and occasional foresight into the future, had a dream the night before Trent passed that she, myself, and our group of friends were surrounding a male who was sick. She thought it was another man in our group because he was older and had leg and foot surgeries and chronic pain. But after she learned of Trent's passing, she knew it was him.

Two weeks later, my two college roommates, Jamie and Kimmi, who are two of my dearest friends to this day, flew in from Pennsylvania and South Carolina to stay with me. I don't think they were prepared for the state they would find me in. Their strong, feisty, independent friend was shattered and broken, wearing Trent's oversized T-shirts, no makeup, eyes swollen, frail and skinny from not eating and barely able to walk. Walking and working out together was something we'd done together since college. So I was inspired by them showing up to help me to get outside and take Rudy on a walk. As I was putting on my tennis shoes, I heard Trent's voice in my head saying, "Babe, are you going to show them the rock?" I hadn't planned to walk that far since walking across the room required a lot of energy at that time. But we walked, one step (one bite) at a time to the rock. It was probably the slowest paced walk we'd ever walked together in twenty-five years, but we did it. It would be a week or two later that I would venture out by myself to get to my strength rock all on my own and encounter the deer, where I would be awakened by animals (more on this in chapter 5).

December 2, 2012 was a pivotal day of my awakening and transformation. It was the one month anniversary of Trent's passing. I woke up wondering, as I had many days, how I was going to get through. Days and weeks had somehow turned into an entire month and I was still in shock. Oprah had recently launched her own channel and I had been tuning in each Sunday for SuperSoul Sunday to be fed, enlightened, and inspired. A place to go for "thought provoking, eye opening, and inspiring conversation. It's food for your soul!" SuperSoul Sunday has not only been all of those things for me, it's been a big part of my transformation and healing.

I can't recall the many details of the Sunday mornings after Trent passed until that Sunday, but Louise Hay and Cheryl Richardson were that day's guest teachers. I'd never heard of either of them before, but I would forever be changed by their messages, particularly Louise Hay's. Louise was speaking about healing your heart and healing your life after loss. I was mesmerized, hanging on to every word. I don't remember the details, but what spoke to me was when Louise talked about how losing someone can open us up to why we are really here, and we ask ourselves how can we serve others. Having been broken down and broken open, I was seeking to understand and know more about why I was still here, seeking within to get still and just listen. What came to me instantly, as if an overwhelming thought or answer was revealed, was that I felt called to serve others to feel, heal, and live better through health and fitness. As a result of finding comfort, healing, and hope through healthy living and strength through fitness, I knew this was the formula to help live our best, healthiest, happiest, and most inspired lives. I started to feel more energetic, alive, and hopeful that I could go on, heal my life, and build a new life of service.

I was inspired to take two immediate action steps. I had to learn more about Louise Hay's work, so I went on Amazon to order one of her books and her *Powerful Thoughts* card deck, which I still use today in my coaching practice with clients. I then called one of Trent's CrossFit Coaches, Billie Rodgers, who had become a family friend and who showed up from out of town to attend Trent's Celebration of Life Service. I asked him to tell me the good, the bad, and the ugly about being a fitness trainer. He said 50 percent is the actual fitness training and the other half is listening and coaching. He said, "Susan, from what I know of you, you've already got the skills to coach and help people. Why don't you start with getting your CrossFit certification?" What? My CrossFit certification? The thought of that seemed out of reach considering I had barely moved the last month. After finding myself struggling to simply walk across the kitchen, I forced myself to head to our basement for an intense, but short, workout. It was the first day that I didn't cry and I knew I wanted and needed more of that feeling. But go for my CrossFit certification? In that moment, Billie had inspired me to think bigger and get up off my ass and off the couch, where what looked like a permanent indention was being made by me sitting there every day. After we hung up the phone, I researched CrossFit certification courses near Indianapolis and found one in Louisville, Kentucky, at the end of January and signed up for it. Boom, just like that, I took a leap of faith (one big bite), not worried about how I was going to get there, just knowing with everything in me that this was the direction I was being called.

The next day would bring more divine intervention. An example of what preacher and televangelist, Joel Osteen, teaches us is a *"Godincidence"*, not a coincidence. One of my friends had planned to visit and bring lunch. People were still bringing food and visiting a month later, which blew me away. Shereen was another soul sister I had shared spiritual conversations and beliefs with. We had just begun to really get to know each other a few months back and had spent time together at a work convention that past September having meaningful conversations about life, relationships, work and more. The convention was in California, so my friend Dorothy had come to visit and stay with me at the hotel for a night. Shereen and Dorothy clicked instantly and had a lot in common as many of my close circle of friends from all walks of life do.

Shereen arrived on that Monday like a beautiful ray of sunshine, with her golden hair and big shining smile. That day she had a light about her that I hadn't seen before. She had been one of those unexpected people that had kept showing up, constantly checking in on me, lifting me up. She presented me with a gift bag that had two books and a card deck, all by none other than Louise Hay. Are you serious? I had just said the day before that I had to learn more about Louise Hay and here comes Shereen with two of her books and another one of her card decks. When I told her about what happened the day before and how I'd just learned of Louise Hay, her work and ordered one of her books and card decks we both got chills and knew that a higher power was working behind the scenes. I was becoming awakened to the possibilities, stronger with each day, yet still raw and weak with emotion and stricken with grief. But I was starting to see not just a new normal, but one that I could actually get excited and smile about. Feelings I didn't think I would ever have again. Mark Nepo says, "Happiness is the joy we experience when striving toward our potential." I was striving toward my new potential and experiencing joy again—one bite at a time.

In the days that followed, I would pull out one of Louise Hay's affirmation cards at times when I needed strength and was seeking help from above. Every single time I would pick the card that spoke exactly to what I was needing and asked for at the time. I was learning about the healing power of positive affirmations and how God and the Universe are always supporting us, especially when we are aware and awakened to the possibilities.

I also started going to one of the local CrossFit gyms that Trent had belonged to in preparation for my weekend in Louisville to earn my certification. I was in awe of the physical strength of the women who trained at the CrossFit gym. I was still gaining back my basic strength and these women were bench pressing massive amounts of weight and performing unassisted pull-ups. I was still uneasy in public, lost, frail and insecure, feelings I now know to be part of the post-traumatic stress disorder I was experiencing.

After one of the warm-ups, we were asked to partner up and perform rounds as part of our WOD (workout of the day). A nice woman named Kelly could see that I was new and unsure of what to do and offered to be my partner. I remember her bright curly blond hair as I spotted her at the bench press. Something about her seemed slightly familiar but I wasn't in a space to think or ask. Over the next couple of weeks, Kelly would become a kind, welcoming face that helped put me at ease when I showed up for the challenging workout sessions.

On the evening of December 23, 2012, I was awakened in the middle of the night, shaken by a dream I'd had where Trent had pushed Kelly's face toward me telling me who she was. It turns out that Kelly was the EMT who showed up at our home the morning Trent collapsed—the one who was trying to calm me down and was ultimately with him in the ambulance when he took his last breath. My grief had erased my memory of her until that moment. I burst into tears with the message I'd received. Though I had not planned to go to the CrossFit gym the next morning, on Christmas Eve, I couldn't wait to get there and talk to Kelly. I didn't get much sleep the rest of that night and headed to the gym in the morning. I knew Kelly usually came at a certain time. It was snowing and the roads were bad, but I was determined to find Kelly and ask her if she knew who I was and if Trent was able to speak before he took his last breath.

Kelly didn't appear on Christmas Eve, as I'd hoped. When I arrived at the gym, the owner Bryn confirmed what Trent had showed me in my dream, and I again broke down into tears, trembling and unable to do the workout. I asked Bryn if he thought Kelly knew who I was and he said she may know but wouldn't have brought it up unless I asked. I would not ever see Kelly again at the CrossFit gym where our paths had crossed in my quest for strength and healing.

About two years later, I finally found the courage to stop in and visit the fire department around the corner from our house where I knew Kelly worked and where the ambulance had come from that fateful morning. But she had moved on. I gave one of the firemen my card and he said he would let her know I stopped by and wanted to speak with her. Another bite taken to heal. To this day, I haven't had the opportunity to speak with Kelly to thank her and ask her what I need for closure, but I will never again forget her face or her gentle, kind spirit.

CHAPTER 2

Lesson: Making Tough Choices For The Right Reasons Always Works Out For The "Even Better"

> "Put your ass where your heart wants to be."
>
> —Steven Pressfield

ONE THING I know for sure is that no matter how much we think we have it all together or how strong we think we are, until we are broken down, brought to our knees, and broken open, we often can't discover our true strengths, gifts or talents, passions and, for many of us, our divine purpose. What I've also learned in my transformation as stated so beautifully by Mark Nepo is that "To be broken is no reason to see all things as broken" and that "whatever opens us isn't as important as what opens within us." When we're broken down or living in fear of all the what-ifs while making a tough or scary decision, our fears can hold us back. But when we make that scary decision for the right reasons, it—life, love, finances, career—all comes back to us, often even better than we could have imagined.

We will all be shaken down to our knees at some point in our lives. To truly transform, we must ensure that we don't define ourselves by what broke us open, but rise up to what is being opened in us as a result. What we do with our suffering or life changing event is what's really important. As Richard Rohr has said, "If you don't transform your suffering, you will transmit it (in unhealthy ways)." Have you ever met people who says their cancer was the best thing that ever happened to them? That they're better because of having had cancer? This is what it means to rise up to what opens within us when we are broken open and down. What Harvard researcher and author Shawn Achor refers to as "post-transformational growth." More on that later.

Downsized, Divorced and Death

For me, this has happened at least twice in my life. Actually, three if I count the first time in my early twenties, which was nothing compared to what I would face later in life. I laugh when I think back to that time and the aha moment that got me back up after what I thought was the worst thing that had ever happened to me. I had just been "downsized" from my first real job in advertising and marketing with a small PR firm. I thought I was going to have a meeting with my boss for a raise and was informed that I was being let go. I lived in an apartment with two roommates and had rent and car payments. After ranting to my friends about how unfair it was that I was let go, I quickly secured two jobs to cover my bills. One, as a waitress at night and the other was working at a museum part time so I could have time to look for my new "real job." I was devastated, embarrassed and felt like all my hopes and dreams for my future and my career were over. It was May of 1995, the month of my twenty-fifth birthday. I had asked for the day off, but was put on the schedule to work at the restaurant. I felt like a complete failure on my twenty-fifth birthday. The next day, I decided I was going to stay in bed and cry about it. Looking for sympathy and someone to share in my pity party, I called my friend and mentor Billie Dragoo who had just started her own business, and who would thrive on to become a nationally award winning entrepreneur recognized for her advocacy work for women. What she said would echo in my head for years to come when I needed it. When I called Billie crying and started to talk about how pathetic my life was, she stopped me midsentence and said with a big commanding sigh, "Get out of bed and be somebody!"

Well, that stopped me in my tracks. Even though it wasn't what I expected or wanted to hear at the time, it was exactly what I needed to hear. It was a big aha moment—a game-changing life-transforming moment. So I did just that. I got out of bed, putt my ass where my heart was and took action to create my new normal and be somebody. Somebody better than a victim of circumstance. Somebody who could create a new normal and transform into who I had set out to be after I graduated college. Somebody who was better as a result of being knocked down. I secured two jobs to pay my rent, car payment and cover the rest of my bills while I followed my heart and put my ass to work, seeking out marketing opportunities. Two months later I landed what to this day is still one of my favorite jobs, as a beverage brand manager for a flavor company. By following and putting my ass where my heart was, I regained my confidence and faith in my abilities and embraced my new gig, which was even better than I could have imagined at the time.

The second life changing event was when I got divorced.

I've found myself over the years since the tragic 9/11 terrorist attacks sharing my personal life lesson experience of how when we make decisions with pure intentions and for the right reasons, it all comes back to us. Usually even better and more than we could have imagined. Though I lived in the Midwest and did not personally know anyone who perished in the 9/11 attacks, I was still heartbroken for everyone who lost someone that day and for our country as a whole. As a new mom, it frightened me to think about the world my daughter would grow up in.

About a week after the horrific attacks by the Taliban on the United States on September 11, 2001, my then husband called me in a panic in the middle of the day at work to say, "We need to talk." OK, I thought. What's up? I didn't want to wait until I got home to find out what he seemed so anxious about. I insisted he tell me. He blurted out that he didn't want to have any more kids and that he was stressed out about finances. Boom, just like that, I had an overwhelming feeling and a big aha moment—I knew my marriage was ending (and that I wasn't *in* love with him, even though I loved him very much). I knew that I could no longer live in a stress-filled home, feeling like I was walking on eggshells, and that no one but a doctor would tell me that I wouldn't have any more children. I had struggled with infertility and had finally conceived and given birth to my daughter, Sophia, who was only fifteen months old at the time. I had also just started a new job four months prior so I could have more flexibility and time with Sophia, which meant I also took a big pay cut, much to my husband's dismay, but it was the tradeoff for more time with my daughter, achieving the work-life balance I wanted, and becoming the kind of mom I wanted to be. When I was on maternity leave embracing every minute with my newborn, I kept thinking of other occupations I was qualified for that offered more flexibility. Becoming a Fitness Trainer was one I was interested in, even back then, but my husband was not supportive of the idea or the start-up pay cut. In my previous job, where I loved the work and my boss, I had worked in a marketing department of mostly men who had stay-at-home wives. So traveling and getting home to take care of the kids wasn't something my colleagues had to manage. When the time for annual reviews came in December of 2000, I received a high review and a pay raise. I then asked for a flexible work schedule and time off or to work from home one day a week in lieu of more money. My boss, Jim, who was supportive and to this day is a dear friend, presented my request and proposal outlining the benefits to companies when offering flexible work schedules and work-from-home options for working mothers. Even though I worked until the Friday before the Sunday that I gave birth, a scheduled C-section, and had a proven track record of high performance, it didn't matter. My request was nixed by the all-male upper management. It was a no go. I was disappointed, but knew that in a male-dominated, strict corporate environment, it was up to me to figure it out and find a way. In April of 2001, I received a call from my former counterpart Matt, who had left the company a month prior to be a sales director at a real estate company. He, by the way, was making much more than I was in the same brand manager position, reaffirming that women were not paid equally at my company and that valuing working mothers was not on the radar. Knowing my desire for a flexible work schedule, he called to tell me about a newly created position at his new company that he thought I would be perfect for. He said I could work four days a week and have a flexible work schedule as long as I made my sales goals. Also, they were located five minutes from my house. I was currently commuting thirty minutes each way. The kicker was that it was a sales and business development position. "No, thank you" was my first reaction. We both worked in marketing together and prided ourselves on being the cornerstone of the business, as we liked to believe the marketing department was. I'd said I'd never get into sales or "sell out." Ha! Never say never. I thought, what do I have to lose? The package sounded perfect, so why not go for the interview? So, I agreed to a meeting with the woman I would be reporting to and it was an instant connection. Meeting Tracy that day forever changed my life and I am eternally grateful for her and my almost twelve years at CENTURY 21 Scheetz. Looking back, I believe it was divine intervention and part of the plan for my life's path. When I turned in my resignation letter, I was excited for my new opportunity to work four days a week along with a flexible work schedule where eyes weren't following me when I walked out of the office at 5:00 p.m. to get home to my baby girl. The significant pay cut didn't bother me, but it became an issue in my marriage. Money wasn't important to me; time with my daughter was. That still hasn't changed to this day. I really loved working with Jim, and though I wasn't exactly excited to go work in real estate, my gut told me it was the right decision. To this day, I know it couldn't have been more right. I was exactly where I was meant to be.

Although Sophia's dad and I weren't talking about trying to have another child at the time, it was something we had talked about in the beginning of our relationship. I had always dreamed of having a big family with at least two or three children of my own. As an adopted child, I yearned for a biological child to experience how my own bloodline might look and resemble me in some way. What features and mannerisms of mine would be carried on? What would a biological child of mine look like? So, when what felt like a 911 emergency call during the middle of the work day came from my then husband, I felt like someone kicked me in the gut and awakened me to knowing I could no longer go on in my unhealthy marriage. This was the "brick" for me. We had been to counseling when Sophia was only four months old. I almost had broken off our engagement twice because of the very same issues that would end our marriage. I didn't want our daughter to grow up in a toxic, volatile environment with her parents fighting and seeing her mother being yelled at on a regular basis. After just a week of discussions, I made the decision to leave. I didn't feel that he truly loved me because he only fought with me and not *for* me or our marriage. Everyone in America was getting back together right after 9/11 as I was leaving my marriage with a baby on my hip and a recent big pay cut. People thought I was crazy and I knew it. Most didn't understand. But I didn't care. I was in survival mode and knew there had to be a better way.

Our divorce was final in three months, on December 28, 2001. I was saddened and in disbelief that this was my life. I loved Sophia's father. He was and is a good person, but we couldn't make it work and I was losing myself. During those three months, I moved out and bought a small house. The perfect little home for Sophia and me, one that I still love and holds some of my best memories to this day. While I was figuring out how to be a single mom with a baby and still learning my new job, my ex-husband found himself a girlfriend and married her the next year. I felt so easily replaced. Although it was hard, it confirmed that I had made the right move. So I continued to move on, one day at a time, one bite at a time.

Within two years, I was thriving at my new sales job. My earnings became more than my salary at my former company. After another year, I'd doubled what I had been making at my marketing job, something that would have never happened had I stayed. About that time, my ex said he made a big mistake in getting married so quickly. They remained married for eight years. I actually cried when he announced their divorce because his wife was very good to Sophia and it saddened me to see Sophia go through the dissolution of another family unit. He would remarry yet again and that story continues to change.

The moral of the story is that when we make decisions for the right reasons, it all comes back to us. The Universe always gives us what we need—usually, more than we ever dreamed of or imagined. When we let go of our fear for the unknown or "what if's worries" and choose faith, choose courage over comfort and stay true to ourselves, it always works out. Usually even better than before. I didn't change jobs for the money, but I gained financially because I was doing something I'd come to love. I was also much happier, after rediscovering myself and getting my confidence back following my divorce. I was living my truth. It's empowering to take care of a house, a full-time career, and a child all on your own. I loved my new life and was growing and transforming into who I was meant to be.

Trading In the Suits for the Sneakers

So when life hit me hard again, the hardest yet, breaking me open and down to my knees on November 2, 2012, the day my husband collapsed at the foot of our bed and suddenly passed away, I was faced with many choices of how to get through and go on. One thing I knew for sure is that I couldn't go back to doing the same job, even though I loved my company, my boss, and the people I worked with. Part of surviving the tragedy of losing Trent was that I had to do something more meaningful, get closer to discovering my true purpose, and find a way to serve others. I remember people saying not to make any big changes or decisions for at least a year. I still can't relate to that idea. Although it may work for some people, it wouldn't have worked for me. My whole life changed when I lost Trent. To keep everything else the same and try to cope would have been harder for me than making changes. How could I keep everything around me the same when everything felt so different? I was forced to create a new normal. For me, that meant I had to make some big changes, sooner rather than later.

So I decided to leave the corporate world after twenty years—losing my six-figure income, health insurance, 401K, a car allowance, and other benefits—to start my own business. Losing these things didn't compare to losing my husband and the life we had, so it was no longer a scary choice. Once again, people thought I was crazy. Not just crazy, but some feared I was mentally and emotionally unstable. In addition to being concerned for my well-being, those close to me weren't quite sure what to do with me. I'd lost weight from a lack of interest in food and most other things, and I'm a girl who loves to eat! For the first couple of months after Trent passed, I lived in sweat pants and Trent's T-shirts, not wearing makeup, and unconcerned for my personal hygiene, hiding in my house, not wanting to leave or get out and see people. Under-eye concealer replaced my usual lipstick as my main staple, and dry shampoo replaced washing my hair every other day. Simple everyday activities like going to the grocery store were difficult. I was weak, foggy, and numb from inactivity and grief. I was suffering from post-traumatic stress disorder and didn't realize it. So when I was faced with having to go back to where I had worked for almost twelve years in January, I knew my heart and head wasn't in it, but I felt obligated to try to see if I could "get it back." I wasn't sure what "it" really was, but I knew in order to survive and go on, I needed to continue getting stronger and helping others find internal strength through health and fitness, and feeling that with every fiber of my being this was my true purpose. At forty-three, I was taking a huge leap of faith that I can only attribute to God leading me through and showing me signs, nudging and assuring me that all would be well. I chose love over fear as a survival tactic and a deep belief that I not only should but also must follow. My dear, sweet dad expressed his concern and asked if I thought I might be too old to work in the fitness business. One of my best friends Jacqueline, known for her tough but unconditional love, discouraged me and said she worried I'd regret it because I wasn't in a state of mind to make such a big decision and leave *everything* I had. To me, I'd already lost everything when I lost Trent, the life we shared and my identity. I'd been through the worst, so if it didn't work out, I knew I could handle it. I also knew somehow that my new endeavor would in fact work out and that it would be just the beginning of rediscovering my path and purpose—the beginning of my new life.

On February 1, 2013, I officially said good-bye to the corporate world that I'd thrived in for twenty years, and started Inspired By Fitness™ out of my basement, my own little health coaching and training business. I was inspired by fitness to get strong again and live on. Three years later, I'm still humbled with gratitude for the work I've been able to do and the people I've been able to serve to get healthier and live their best lives. I now earn more than my starting income, although nowhere near six figures, and I'm perfectly OK with that. You can't put a price on serving others, doing what you love on your own terms, achieving a work-life balance that works for you, discovering and living out your purpose. I truly believe God brings me each person I'm meant to serve through Inspired By Fitness, whether for six weeks or three years. I know this is just the beginning and a platform of what's to come. And again, a lesson that teaches us that when we make decisions choosing love over fear and with the right intentions, the Universe supports us and it all comes back to us. More than we ever dreamed of!

Starting my own business was more than a leap of faith. It was, and still is today, my self-prescribed grief therapy. It is still today, on those emotionally tough days, my reason and purpose to get out of bed. On those tough days, I find that each time I finish a client session, I have renewed energy and I always feel better, more fulfilled, whole and happier, even when I get up at 5:00 a.m. to get ready for my first morning client.

When I returned to work, two months after Trent passed, to the company I'd worked for and the people who had been so good to me for almost twelve years, I knew I needed to do something with this calling I felt to serve others through health and fitness. Exercise, prayer, and positive affirmations became my grief therapy and my new spiritual practice. I was inspired by fitness to find strength within to get out of bed and get through the days in my darkest hours. I was inspired by fitness to create my new normal and live my best life without Trent. And, I was inspired by fitness to take a leap of faith to quit my job and leave the corporate world after twenty years to help others live their best life through health and fitness; to find strength, healing and purpose in their own lives; to create a lifestyle of overall wellness to include not just physical fitness, but emotional, mental, intellectual, and spiritual fitness. This is what Inspired By Fitness encompasses and is still the essence of my coaching and professional and spiritual practice.

When I first returned to work, I wanted to see if I could get back the comfort, desire and confidence I'd had in working in my old business world. My company had been so good to me, I wanted to at least try to go back and make it work. Day after day, I would force myself to put on my big girl heels and dress up for work. A ritual that was surprisingly difficult as I no longer had the desire to dress up, wear makeup, and be a corporate girl. Those who knew me and those I'd worked with over the years were used to me always looking professional, styled, accessorized, and dressed for success. I'd always loved fashion and dressing up. For the first time in twenty years, I found myself with no desire for fashion and not wanting to play that part anymore. It meant nothing to me and I just wanted to put on my yoga pants and trade in my suits for sneakers. I struggled with Trent not being there each morning to see me out the door and revel in what I was wearing. He loved my "look" and would call me at work on days he would leave the house before me to ask me what I was wearing and how I was wearing my hair. We were that connected every day and as madly in love until the very end as we were when we first met. The "honeymoon phase" never ended for us.

Returning to my old workplace meant facing leaving the house without kissing Trent good-bye, as I had every single morning. It meant commuting to and from work without our daily phone calls. It meant returning to a place and business world where everything else remained the same, when I was now so very different. I felt out of place and no longer in my element. I'd lost my confidence and didn't want to see people for fear I'd cry or that they would look at me with pity. I struggled to breathe at times. I felt like my world was turned upside down, but everyone else was going on the same. I knew I couldn't be in that world and function the way I used to. I knew I had to find my way along a whole new path.

After two weeks back at Scheetz, I sat down with my boss, with tears streaming down my face as I told her I didn't think I was doing the company justice and that I couldn't continue working for the company. Getting it out and saying it was the hardest part. I was slowly finding strength through showing vulnerability. Another thing I would have never done before—express vulnerability and be totally OK with it. It was a part of my transition. I don't think she was surprised and probably had been waiting for me to come to terms, make a decision, and just say it. She was once again amazing and supportive, just as she'd always been to me. We agreed she would make the announcement and that I would write a letter of departure, my good-bye. Here is that letter:

To My Dear Colleagues, Friends and Scheetz Family,
Jan. 24, 2013

Where do I start but to begin with Thank You...although somehow thank you doesn't't seem like enough sometimes, I am forever grateful to our entire company and every one of you who have reached out to help support me and my family (Sophia, Matt and Joe) through the sudden, unexpected and unbearable loss of my husband, Trent. I was, and continue to be blown away by the overwhelming outreach of support from everyone at Scheetz. From the very moments after I arrived at the hospital room while they were still working on bringing him back to the hours that followed at our home, it was my Scheetz family that was right by my side, along with my family and friends in the hours, days and weeks that followed.

I truly appreciate each and every card, note, call, letter, book, journal, text, FaceBook message/post, prayer and hug. I've always known that at Scheetz, we have something special—the people and genuine care, concern and support—but I never expected the tremendous outreach from not just those of you that I have grown to know well over my 11 1/2 years, but from those of you that I haven't had the opportunity to work with or know as well. Even my friends and family were in awe of how my "company and work friends" showed up, picked me up (literally), reached out and continue to help as I move forward day by day. One thing I know for sure is that there aren't many companies today in corporate America that support one another and show up the way our people do at CENTURY 21 Scheetz. It is a true privilege and blessing to be associated with each and every one of you, so thank you.

As I move forward, I'm coping day by day, sometimes hour by hour to figure out my "new normal" and our life without him. For me, everything has changed and things that were once important and/or that once drove me are no longer. As I started to face coming back to work, I was faced with getting out of bed for a purpose other than for my kids and asking myself what am I really passionate about? What is healing to me? What brings me happiness? What inspires me?

I knew in my heart then and I now know that my professional journey must continue, as part of my new normal, outside of corporate America, and outside of the company that I have loved and given my best to for almost 12 years. I know I can no longer serve with the desire, drive or commitment that not only my current position & this company deserves but that I must move on to best serve myself and my healing journey.

I've grown through some of the most critical years of my life during my time at Scheetz and it has been some of the best and most fun years. So it is with mixed emotions that I move forward to follow my heart and my passion in the only way that I know how—helping & healing others through Health & Fitness Training, as it was working out to get emotionally strong again that began to heal me, give me hope and inspire me to live on and live my new best life.

It is my hope that I can be an "alumni" member of Scheetz and is my commitment to be there for any of you who think I can help you in any way, whether it's simply staying connected, sharing LinkedIn tips or getting together for lunch, coffee or a workout! ☺
With love and gratitude,
Susan Van Hoosen

When I left Scheetz at the end of January 2013, I had about three months of savings in the bank. I didn't have much of a business plan. I figured I should work on my marketing and logo design, develop my website, and continue my new professional training. I had just finished earning my CrossFit Level 1 Trainer Certification and planned to work on earning a nationally accredited certification through ACE (American Council in Exercise) in the next few months.

To my surprise, as soon as I announced I was launching my own fitness training business, my friend Zaida asked if she could be my first client and start right away. Divine messages continued to guide me and show up like a silent business partner. One evening after one of my first training session with Zaida, I shared that I was working on design concepts for my business logo. I mentioned that I wanted to incorporate an elephant (in honor of

Trent's "How Do You Eat An Elephant? One Bite At A Time" saying) as part of my logo design and asked what she thought, since elephants aren't exactly the epitome of fitness. She said she loved the idea and that it wasn't as crazy as I might think. I told her I planned to research images of elephants the next couple of days and hire a graphic designer. The very next day, I received a letter from my friend Robin who worked at the Indianapolis Zoo inviting me and the kids for a special visit at the zoo. Included was this picture of an elephant named Sophie, age forty six. An elephant named Sophie, my daughter's name, and one who is age forty six, the age Trent had just turned three weeks before he passed on. That's what we call a "Godincidence", not a coincidence.

Notice her **strong physique & beautiful curves, the trunk pointing up signifying happiness and the inspirational waterfall, which to me is heavenly.** A sign from heaven. I remember not knowing whether to laugh or cry when I saw this picture. I was giddy with belief and in some ways disbelief at how the Universe was speaking to me, answering any doubts I might have had. "Ok, I get it. The answer is yes, I should absolutely feature an elephant in my logo!", I recall saying out loud, looking up. Once again feeling completely connected and guided.

Two weeks later, while I was taking a Pilates class, a sweet young girl named Hayley, who I'd met in class, said she overheard me talking about being a trainer and working from my home and asked if I would train her. Just like that, in two weeks I had my first two clients. Not what I expected! Within three months, I had six more clients all from friends, neighbors, and referrals who reached out to ask if I could help them. I knew from the very beginning that this was God's handy work and that He was sending me each person I was meant to help, whether I thought I was ready or not! Almost three years later, this is still how my business has grown and continues to evolve. I don't advertise or solicit business. I prefer having others share their stories of how I've helped them with their friends and family.

When I met with my former boss (and company president) a few months after launching Inspired By Fitness, she asked me what my business plan was. Coming from a world of being measured by metrics, sales numbers, and growth goals, it was a natural question. Without hesitation, I recall smiling and replying with, "My business plan each day is to get out of bed and be somebody (thank you, Billie) and serve others the best way I know how. Hopefully, the rest will come and so far it's working." Not an answer she was expecting or one that she knew how to process, but the only one that made any sense at the time. I knew she probably thought I was crazy and I was completely OK with that.

Although most of my family and friends believed in me and my new endeavor, I'm not sure any of us imaged that my little, under the radar, home-based training business that quietly started in my basement would grow into what it is today, where I coach multiple clients at my studio and work onsite with my corporate clients each week. Not an empire by any means, but bigger at this stage than I ever imagined. Within a year and a half after starting Inspired By Fitness, I earned four training certifications including my ACE Personal Trainer, ACE Health Coach, TRX Trainer, and TRX Sports Medicine Certification. I poured myself into my work and education and people continued to come, week after week. I'm still amazed on many days when I prepare for the number of people who actually come to my home-based business for training and coaching; people I get to serve and work with. When someone falls off the client roster, I don't worry the way I used to in the corporate world. Earlier, I would have looked at these moments—when a client discontinues or needs to stop coming for whatever reason—as failure and lost income. Now I simply see it as our work together having lived its course and served its purpose and as God giving me time to rest and prepare for the next person I'm meant to help. I was able to make a comeback by not going back. As SuperSoul guest, minister, and life coach Tim Storey says, "A comeback is not a go back." I couldn't go back to my old life and work where everything was the same when I had become so different. I was able to transform my life and make a comeback by choosing to not go back. By making the tough choice with pure intentions for the right reasons, it all came back to me, even better than before and even bigger than I could have imagined.

Although I operate the entire business on my own, I know that I'm not *on my own* in the work I do. I know with everything in me that God is blessing my work and nudging people to reach out to me for help. I know that when I pray to God and Archangel Michael for strength and energy and to Archangel Gabriel to help me communicate and inspire those I serve, that they are with me, helping me along and blessing my work. I know that Trent is guiding me, as I felt him do from the beginning. I started early on believing and reciting the scripture Philippians 4:13 out loud, "I can do all things through He who strengthens me." This is still one of my go-to prayers, one of many affirmations that carry me through each day.

In fact, when I look back, I can see now that in one of my darker, scarier moments thirteen years ago, I was drawn to this scripture to help carry me through after my divorce. I remember being in Macy's just after the new year, so it must have been 2002, pushing Sophia's stroller and being drawn to a shiny cross necklace. It was in the fine jewelry department and they were having a 70 percent after-Christmas sale. I didn't have much money and I had never spent more than one hundred dollars on jewelry before, but I felt compelled to "invest" in that diamond cross necklace with the blue stone in the middle as a symbol of the strength I needed to get through my new life as a newly divorced mom of a toddler. Still reeling from the pain and disbelief of where life was taking me, and feeling alone, I remember thinking I needed the cross necklace to remind me that I can do all things through He who strengthens me. I think the necklace only cost about $150, which was a lot of money for me at the time, but it was a gift I gave myself, in more ways than one.

With the necklace would come one of those miracle stories thirteen years later. I'm not exactly sure when it happened but I lost my cross necklace sometime between 2005 and 2006. For years I searched and wondered where it could have gone. I'm ashamed to say that I even wondered if someone took it. I couldn't understand how it could disappear when I always hung my necklace in my jewelry box. Over the years, every now and then, I would think about the necklace and remember fondly the strength it gave me and what it represented, still saddened that it had disappeared. And then came one of those unexplained miracles.

At the beginning of October 2015, I had been asking for more help from above to help me move through my grief—what I refer to as my biggest, hardest season of grief. October starts the three week marathon of anniversary dates that are the hardest. Trent's birthday is October 13. Our wedding anniversary is October 27 and November 2 is the date he passed. And then, of course, follows Thanksgiving and the Christmas holiday season. Thinking about facing another round of these dates and holidays causes my grief to erupt, usually surfacing as fatigue, sadness, and neck and upper back pain—the body's way of dealing with what we suppress. Last year during this time, I started to notice signs of what would later be diagnosed as the onset of psoriasis, a skin condition that can be triggered at a later age by stress, hormones, or an emotional event. Of course, when the psoriasis started to appear on the back of my neck and later around my belly button, I thought the worst and thought it might be skin cancer. Knowing that dis-ease causes disease, I decided I couldn't deal with it and had to get through the holidays first, so it wasn't until early January that I finally went to see the dermatologist who diagnosed my psoriasis. Although not happy with the psoriasis diagnosis, I was relieved that it wasn't skin cancer. Thankfully topical medications and healthy living have kept it at bay.

So as I prepared to make myself extra busy and plan for a fall break getaway to California with Sophia to visit one of my dearest friends, Dorothy, to give us a healthy, fun distraction for the season ahead, I prayed for help to get through. On the first Saturday in October, I was putting clothes away in my closet and my eye was drawn to one of my jewelry necklace hangers. At the base of the necklace stand was my cross necklace. In shock, I picked it up and marveled at it wondering how it got there. I knew it wasn't there the day before, or any other time before, so I thought Sophia must have found it and had it all along. But when I asked her where she found it, she didn't know what necklace I was talking about. She had never seen the necklace and she frequently looked through my jewelry. I realized she was too young to remember it from before it disappeared. How could this be, I thought? Then I knew, it was one of those miracles that I had been noticing and open to seeing since my awakening after Trent passed. The only explanation, although some would say not a logical one, is that Spirit or an angel had placed the necklace there; that it was time I got it back to help give me the strength I needed to get through the days ahead. I giggled out loud in awe of what I was realizing. I felt lifted and even more connected to the other side, to Spirit and to God. I truly believe that it was a gift from Archangel Michael and part of his handy work. I haven't taken the necklace off since. When I wrote this, it was October 18, 2015. The following week, another miracle occurred. My next-door neighbor, who had spent the last year and a half complaining to the HOA about me and my business and made every effort to shut me down, called me from work and asked me to put the "For Sale" sign up in their yard for the Realtor. My neighbor thanked me for demonstrating what it means to be a Christian in the midst of the "meanness" and attacks from her soon-to-be ex-husband. God certainly has a sense of humor. I, of all people, who just months before had wished they would move, was being asked by the very people who tried to shut me down to put the "For Sale" sign in their yard. I felt a mix of emotions that included sadness for my neighbors who were getting a divorce and moving; relief, peace, and joy in the validation of my spiritual growth and witnessing again the miracle of when light and love win—and heal—over darkness and fear. One of the many joys of running my own business is that I get to do what I'm called to do, while maintaining the work-life balance I've always strived for. One of the "paybacks" is that I get to create my own schedule and be home with my daughter. I work a lot more hours than I ever have, starting my work day at 6:00 a.m. and finishing around 6:30 p.m. on most weekdays. But it doesn't feel like work. It's just what I do, how I serve, and live out my day. It's part of my spiritual practice and continues to evolve with each and every person that comes to me as a special and unique gift to unwrap, inspire, and grow on our life's journey together. If I could do it for free, I would. That's how much it fulfills me, strengthens, and inspires me. It's my passion and my purpose. I am also beginning to see that this is a platform for what's to come and to the work I have ahead of me; a platform for sharing my story and writing this book. I never imagined after Trent passed, or even a year ago, that I could believe that some of the best is yet to come.

CHAPTER 3

Lesson: How To Leverage Your Super Human Power.

> "My Dear, you've always had the power. You just had to learn it for yourself."
>
> —Glenda the Good Witch, *The Wizard of Oz*

ONE LESSON I'VE learned again and again is that we have to learn the lessons ourselves through experience. And that a lesson is repeated until it's learned. While we are children, our parents, coaches and teachers teach us many valuable lessons, but true wisdom is gained through personal experience, heartbreak, mistakes, setbacks, loss, observations, and how we move forward through the lesson. Learning life's lessons is a big part of why we are here. There are things we can do to make learning the life lessons a lot easier and a lot more fun. We don't always have to learn the hard way once we find our strength and leverage our power within.

Your Superhuman Power

Have you ever been asked the question, "If you could have any super human power, what would it be?" My answer always used to be "either to go undercover being invisible or have the ability to heal people." What I've learned throughout my transformation is that I already have the coolest super human power at my fingertips at all times—my internal power. You have it too! We all do, and once you choose and *seek* to be aware and conscious of this super power, your life can change. You can change your life.

By leveraging our internal power, we can find the strength within to overcome and tackle the tough decisions, challenges, setbacks, crises, and suffering we'll face throughout our life. As I shared in the first two chapters, we can leverage our internal power by first moving forward and taking it one bite at a time and then listening to our gut; following our heart in making choices for the right reasons, responding to the situation with the right intentions, and trusting that it will work out for the "even better."

To simplify, leveraging your internal power means to do a "gut check" and listen to what your gut is silently telling you. To become still and listen for the answers within; following your intuition or "gut instinct," is the internal guide that we all have. Follow your heart and your gut. Ignore the fear-based talk and limiting beliefs in your head or the negative, disempowering people (negative energy) around you. Learn that "no" (from one's gut or another person) usually means "wrong direction" and learn to be open to the possibilities. Remember that your internal power can come from knowing what Philippians 4:13 teaches us: You can do all things through He who strengthens you. Whatever your "He," God, Higher Power, or belief system is, pulling from the belief that you are supported by your higher power helps to believe you can do anything and that all things are possible if you believe it to be.

When I lost my husband, my self-prescribed grief therapy was a blend of finding internal strength through external physical strength, seeking to connect at a higher spiritual level, positive affirmations, and the informal support group of my girlfriends. I knew no one could take my pain away from me, make it all go away or change what had happened. I had to learn how to deal with my grief and move through it on my own. I had to feel it to heal it. In spite of all of the support I had, it was ultimately up to me to get through it, to get out of bed each day and *choose* how to move forward with my life. In creating my new normal, my head was unclear and blurry at times, so I allowed my heart and my gut to lead the way and guide me forward, giving me peace amid the uncertainty of what the future held. I learned from my divorce and other hard times in my life that I had to pull from my internal power—my faith, determination, and gratitude—to crawl out of the darkness and back into the light. Being broken down and broken open taught me to pull from my center, my inner strength and voice, my intuition as my guide. The knowledge and faith that my internal power ruled over whatever I faced externally gave me the super human power I needed to survive, thrive, and go on—one bite at a time.

Today, when asked the question, "What super human power would you have if you could have one?" my answer is still to heal people. For as Dr. Christiane Northrup teaches us, "Every woman who heals herself, helps heal all the women who came before and after her." By leveraging my internal power to serve others to help live their best, healthiest, happiest, most inspired lives, my healing journey continues, and my internal power grows stronger.

The next time you're faced with uncertainty, close your eyes and become still as you look within; let go and release any expectations. The answer will come as you feel it in your gut and your heart speaks to you—the same way you find yourself subconsciously responding when you hear or see something that evokes emotions of sadness, fear, joy, or love by placing your hand on your heart when you see or hear it. You reach toward your heart as you absorb, process, and feel it. You reach internally to respond to the external. It may not be the answer you wanted or expected, but know that whatever comes to you is guiding you from within to leverage you to a higher place.

The Power of Positive Affirmations

You may have heard before that our thoughts become things. The story we tell ourselves becomes our reality, good or bad. We become whatever follows after we say, "I am." As the great, inspiring, late Dr. Wayne Dyer taught us, "Our intention creates our reality." I learned about the power of positive affirmations long before I knew what they were. Since I can remember, I've been an "inspirational quote person." I collected quotes when I was younger and continue to seek inspiration through the power of words and wisdom of others. A while ago, a friend came to visit me at my home for the first time and quickly observed, "You sure have a lot of quotes around." I giggled to myself as I knew it probably wasn't a compliment. For a split second I worried that I may have too many decorative artworks of quotes displayed throughout my home, but that concern quickly went away as I know that my inspirational quotes are what make my home, my home; what make it warm, welcoming, peaceful, and cozy. Cozy is a word I frequently hear when people describe my home. I think the coziness is the comfortable vibe partly made up of the uplifting, inspiring, and affirming words around my home.

I've drawn from quotes not just during life's tough times, but in everyday life. Throughout my corporate life, I would constantly seek out opportunities to hear speakers and attend workshops for professional and personal development, what I referred to as my "inspirational boost."

What I've learned from the beginning of my transformation is the power that positive affirmations can have in our life and how our internal power can be disarmed by negative affirmations. I now teach and share this practice with my coaching clients, in my workshops, with my friends and family, and in my personal life. I refer to it as a practice because, just like any other healthy habit that helps create a sustainable lifestyle of health and overall wellness, we must practice training our mental, emotional, and spiritual wellness. So practice saying, writing, believing, and declaring positive affirmations. It can lift us up. It's how we can release ourselves from negative thought patterns and set ourselves free from limiting beliefs that hold us back. It's as simple as reframing how we don't feel into how we want to feel by rewording the desired feeling or belief into a simple positive statement or mantra. For example, instead of saying (whether out loud or to yourself) "I am worried about…" or "What if it doesn't work out?" practice saying "I am at peace knowing all will be well" or "I am looking forward to a positive outcome." It is much like the positive affirmations I teach my fitness clients to declare: "I am strong, fit, and healthy" instead of "I am fat and out of shape" and "I am making healthier choices each day" instead of "I'm bad or I ate badly or I was awful this week." Simply reframing the words *good* or *bad* to *healthy* or *unhealthy* makes all the difference in not just the health story, but the life story we tell ourselves. It affects how we can draw from our internal power by positively affirming our beliefs and our thoughts. Thus, we can transform our thoughts to create a new positive reality and transform our intention to rise up to our higher self and live our best, healthiest, happiest, most inspired life.

CHAPTER 4

Lesson: Grief Lessons Learned

"In the end, it's not the years in your life that count. It's the life in your years."

- ABRAHAM LINCOLN

ONE THING THAT I know for sure is that grief is an on-going, evolving, individual, and unpredictable emotion and experience. It is a process with no end and no deadline, although some people may want or expect you to have an end to your grief, usually so *they* can feel more comfortable. We will all experience loss at some point. It's a part of life. However, levels of loss are subjective. And until you've experienced the loss of someone that you loved more than you could have ever imagined, whether a spouse, child, parent, sibling, best friend, or "your person," it's difficult to understand or to know what to do when someone you know is suffering from a loss.

In the cycle of life, we may subconsciously expect to lose a grandparent, an older relative, or one day when we're older, outlive our parents simply by the aging process. But, we never expect to lose a child or a parent or a spouse at a young age. I say *young* because I never imagined losing my husband, especially so suddenly. I used to think of widows as older people, in their seventies or eighties, like the television show, *The Golden Girls*. I had never known anyone in their forties or younger who was widowed. Now I know three other widows who live in my own little community, who were all in their forties too when they lost their husbands. I've been blessed to work with and become friends with all three of these amazing women through Inspired By Fitness.

Although each of us are on our own grief journey as widows and in different phases, our journeys are similar and we know that we are the only ones who truly understand some of the emotions, challenges, and downright awful situations that we are faced with in moving forward as young, widowed mothers. Two, three, or even seven years later—it doesn't end, it just changes.

Twenty days after Trent passed, I received what would set the tone for my grieving process. It was a beautiful poem sent by my friend Kristy, whom I worked with. She had lost one of her best friends suddenly by a different kind of tragedy a few years ago, so she had a deeper understanding than others about the state of grief I was in. This is the poem she'd sent to me:

> You can shed tears that he is gone,
> or you can smile because he has lived.

You can close your eyes and pray that he'll come back,
or you can open your eyes and see all he's left.
Your heart can be empty because you can't see him,
or you can be full of the love you shared.
You can turn your back on tomorrow and live yesterday,
or you can be happy for tomorrow because of yesterday.
You can remember him only that he is gone,
or you can cherish his memory and let it live on.
You can cry and close your mind,
be empty and turn your back.
Or you can do what he'd want:
smile, open your eyes, love and go on.

—David Harkins

After bawling when I received her e-mail with no other words than this simple yet heartwarming poem, I wiped away the cleansing tears, printed the poem and placed it in a frame, displaying it in my bathroom for well over two and a half years. Each morning I would awaken to these words. Even on the days when I would cry and lose my mind, feel empty-hearted because I couldn't see him or touch him, or want to turn my back on tomorrow and not face another day without him, the poem would remind me that I must choose to cherish his memory and the love we shared and let it live on, to smile, open my eyes, and go on. Consciously and subconsciously I was being awakened to how I would embrace the process of grief—one bite at a time.

What I've learned about grief is that it's an overwhelming emotion that can change hour by hour, day by day, week by week, and year by year. I first began writing about my grief journey in a blog on my website long before I could bear to write about Trent's passing in my journal. Expressing myself and putting pen to paper in my journal was much harder than typing away on a computer. Writing in my journal was more personal and made it more real than getting it out on a keyboard. When I look back and reread some of the grief blogs I've written, I couldn't remember writing most of the words. I was amazed that I was able to reflect and share such raw emotions, since exposing my vulnerability and feelings of weakness are not something I would have done before my awakening. But as Brene' Brown has taught me, we must dare to show up and be seen. As the subtitle of her book, *Daring Greatly,* states: *The Courage to Be Vulnerable Transforms the Way We Live, Love, Parent and Lead.* Vulnerability is a strength and it has made me stronger and helped transform me. When I try to go back to the first year, it's foggy and dark. Yet there are many crystal-clear moments. So when I read my blogs, I can't believe I was able to write, express, and share what I did at the time. At the time, writing each blog was healing for me. I see now that I was in a state of transformation and allowing myself to be vulnerable gave me strength to feel it and thus heal.

Here are a few of my grief blogs:

Fisher's first football game '12

September 2nd, 2013

*It's been 10 months today since I lost Trent...since we lost Trent and everything changed. Labor Day Weekend is the last national holiday of **getting through the "firsts" of national holidays.** The really big ones are still to come—his birthday, our wedding anniversary and the date he died so suddenly and unexpectedly on the morning of Nov. 2nd, and with each first, whether it's a holiday, going somewhere for the first time without him or doing something that we used to **do without him is*** *always a huge step*. Some are harder than others and some I'm able to do with strength that I know comes from above.

This weekend was rough, significant and a breakthrough all at the same time. In preparation for the holiday weekend while grocery shopping for snacks at the pool, I decided it was **time to buy beer for the first time**...I always had beer on hand for Trent, and I haven't been able to buy it since he passed, but an 18 pack of Coors Lite went into the grocery cart and I felt a sense of accomplishment. For those of you who knew Trent and who really knew us, you'll understand why that was so meaningful. The next day on Friday was the first Fishers Home Football game against HSE—always a big, fun game. **This photo is from last year's opening home game**...entering the stadium without him was difficult but with the power of Sophia and 4 of her friends who came over before the game to get ready, I had a new focus—to make sure these beautiful 13 year old girls were safe and having fun.

As I saw **#49 run out onto the field for the kick-off, I knew how proud and happy Trent would have been to see Joe**, a sophomore, playing on the kick off and wearing his big brother's number. I ached for him to be there, but I knew he was watching from above. When Matt arrived from Ball State and walked out on the field, with the same walk as his father, to be a with a few of last year's graduating football alumni on the sidelines, I felt Trent even more and as much as I yearned for him to be physically there, I found comfort in knowing both boys have the foundation that Trent set for them.

When I awoke today, and looked at his side of the bed as I do every morning—empty, I didn't want to move. *Knowing I could actually sleep in a little because it's Labor Day and knowing I would have to face the 10 month anniversary date made me want to stay in bed all day…thank goodness for dogs…Rudy needed to go out and so I went. Coffee in bed, as Trent and I loved to do and crying it out while Sophia slept so she wouldn't see me cry worked until about 11:00 am, when she got up and saw the tissues on my nightstand. We laid together and cuddled for a few minutes and she said she wanted to go downstairs and fix herself some breakfast. Five minutes later,* **in true, strong, sweet Sophia form, she came upstairs with a tray adorning a candle, a coffee cup with a flower from our yard, trail mix she made for me along with some orange juice and her breakfast. Sad tears turned into "happy tears" of love, joy, support and comfort**…*by noon I felt emotionally drained and knew I didn't want to feel like that all day, so as the sun finally started to shine, I knew I would feel better if I took Rudy on a walk, one step at a time.* **With each step, I started to feel stronger** *and slowly but surely, walking turned into running and as it usually ends up when I go for a walk in an effort to* **move and feel better,** *these walks end up turning into some of my best, most therapeutic runs! As the adrenaline rush set in I* couldn't believe just 20 minutes or so ago I barely had the energy to walk and I knew, once again, **both God and Trent were with me, helping me move forward, literally one step at a time.**

Walking/Running it out and physically working out my emotions IS my grief therapy. Although I don't have the extra physical weight, I have the emotional weight that sometimes feels like an extra 100 pounds weighing me down, bringing me to my knees and sucking the energy from my body…so although I don't have the physical weight to lose, I can relate to my clients and understand what it feels like for anyone who may have weight to lose in order to become healthy or feel better, stronger or more energetic. And I know it makes me a better Trainer. **With each client that I'm blessed to work with, I become stronger along with them because it feeds my spirit and is healing when I know I am helping someone else become stronger, healthier, leaner, more confident, energetic and happy, simply by working out and showing themselves that they CAN DO the very things they think they cannot do.** Eleanor Roosevelt said it best "we must do the very thing we think we cannot do." This can be a game changer, a life changer if we choose to allow it.

Ten Months later, I'm doing things I didn't think I could ever do again or would ever do. I didn't think I could do this life without him…and now I know the only way I'm able to fulfill my purpose and follow my life's path to serve and help others through health and

fitness, is because of him and that his spirit got what it needed in this lifetime, but I still have work to do
   —one step at a time, one day at a time and one bite at a time.

September 14, 2013

 So, I thought going to Joe's first home game at Fishers Tigers Stadium was tough. Then there came Matt's first home game at Ball State and even though he wasn't playing and I couldn't go, the thought of how it might have been with Trent still here made my heart sink in bewilderment that he is really not here for all of this… **Football season, probably Trent's favorite season and one with many treasured, fun memories of not only attending Matt & Joe's games, Trent coaching both boys all through their HSE Youth League days,** *watching college and Colts football on weekends at our home and at our favorite sports pubs.*
 This particular Saturday makes it all surreal. Maybe because it's another "first" I have to get through or maybe because this important and special part of our lives over the years makes me ache for him even more or maybe because I actually really enjoy watching football, thanks to Trent, and there wasn't anyone in the world who I had more fun with and enjoyed hanging out watching

football with more than Trent—ever. Not only did I love hearing his stories from his college football days at Iowa State and what really went on at the bottom of the tackle pile ups, but he was my play-by-play MC so I could really understand what was happening during the game!

Football Season—it makes me think of a Bible verse that I have always loved and now it brings new meaning: **Ecclesiastes 3:1–4 There is a time for everything, and a season for activity under the heavens. A time to be born and a time to die, a time to plant and a time to uproot, a time to kill and a time to heal, a time to tear down and a time to rebuild, a time to weep and a time to laugh, a time to mourn and a time to dance."** *This football season I think about his time on this earth and his time to die, those of us left here—our time to heal, my world being torn down when he died, and being in the process of rebuilding a new life without him, a time to weep as I do often, laugh, mourn and dance—I LOVED his dancing—all at the same time when I think of him... and ultimately smile knowing that we had IT. And, IT was a gift that most people never get in their entire lifetime on earth.*

"A Season To Mourn and A Season To Dance"— **this football season although I continue to mourn, I'm able to laugh, rebuild and dance, just as he would want us to.** *I wish I could say that I first read or heard Ecclesiastes 3:1–4 in church growing up, but I* **actually heard it first read by Kevin Bacon in the movie Footloose**—*gotta love the '80s movies—it struck me then*

and has always stayed with me. Maybe it's coming full circle in a way I can relate to on a deeper level or maybe because I'm so much more in touch with my Spirit and the other side that I know that our life here on Earth is full of these Seasons and it's up to us how we choose to get through each of these important seasons.

After Football Season, I have "our season" to get through—his birthday, our wedding anniversary and the day he passed—all in 3 weeks. A season to mourn, a season to laugh and smile at all of the memories and a season to heal and dance, as he loved to do, remembering his life and how I am better because of him (Trent) and He (God) who strengthens me!

October 13, 2013 Trent's last birthday

Today would have been Trent's 47th Birthday. I could have never imagined that **this photo, one of my favorites of us, would be the last time we celebrated his birthday together** and one of our last photos taken, one year ago today.

Last year for his birthday, I planned a surprise evening to go see one of his newly discovered favorite country artists, Eric Church, live in concert with some friends. Again, our **love for country music was an ongoing theme in our lives, which is why I still can't listen to country mus**ic…not in the car, not at home, not out, not anywhere am I able to listen to country music—yet. One bite at a time with that one for sure and seems small in comparison to the other steps and bites I've been able to take that seem bigger and harder in scale. But, it's just too much right now to listen to country music and still a step I'm just not ready to take.

I recently told a girlfriend that **the fact that I can't listen to country music yet sounded like the title and theme of a good country song** and that maybe I'd just write it!

I'm pretty sure Trent spent his last birthday here in the physical world just as he would have liked to—we started the day by attending Joe's freshman football game in the morning at Fishers Tigers Stadium and went home and did a CrossFit workout together. By 5:00, it was Birthday Happy Hour at our house and two of our friends that we were going to the concert with came over for a birthday cocktail, took this picture and our driver then took us downtown for dinner and the concert.

I always used to tell Trent that **it seemed like God took the best ones first and early in life,** and I'm still wrapping my arms around the fact that he isn't here anymore. But I have peace knowing that he lived his life well, with integrity, honor, respect, love and that he had his priorities in order—family first, his friends and helping others—which is why at **his Celebration of Life Service it was standing room only and grown men shed tears as they spoke of how much Trent impacted their life, what a great friend he was and how much they admired the way he lived, loved and spent time with his family…** Not about how much money he made or how successful he was in the business world for he was successful in life, *love, family, authentic friendships and what really matters in life.*

Preparing for today and spending another first, his birthday without him was a choice—and I chose to plan a weekend doing just what he would have wanted with loving and supportive friends by our side—*Joe's football game Friday night, Matt's football game at Ball State yesterday, connecting with my spiritual group this afternoon and dinner out tonight with Joe and Sophia at one of Trent's favorite restaurants (and one of our special places) to celebrate his life and honor his memory.*

My friend Kathy is also running her very first marathon in Chicago today and in addition to achieving this tough physical, mental and emotional challenge in honor of her son Scott, another beautiful life lived and lost too young, who passed away unexpectedly almost 10 years ago, **she is also running in honor of Trent's Birthday and a little girl named Rachel who is battling her own illness. Scott, Trent and Rachel will give her strength to keep going, step by step, one mile (stone) at a time, just like I have to do every day—One Bite At A Time.**

Happy Birthday Babe—I Love You, "Always and Forever"!

February 2, 2014

I realized earlier this week that Feb. 1st would be the 1-year Anniversary of when **I officially formed INSPIRED BY FITNESS**, *LLC. and that one year ago this weekend is also when I traveled to Lexington, KY to earn my CrossFit Certification and become a* **CrossFit Level 1 Certified Trainer**. *Three months later in early May after intense studying and training, I earned my* **ACE (American Council of Exercise) Personal Trainer Certification** *and that following July, I traveled to Louisville, Kentucky, to earn my* **TRX Certification**. *During that time, I was blessed with people reaching out to me, since I wasn't advertising, to ask if I could help them improve their fitness and health, each in their own way and all with unique needs of improved internal and external strength, just as I was working on as part of my grief therapy in choosing this meaningful work. I felt then and I still believe that* **God has brought and will continue to bring me each and every person and opportunity** *I am meant to help and serve through INSPIRED BY FITNESS.*

When I left my job of almost twelve years last January 2013, two months after Trent suddenly passed and after returning and trying to make it work and see if I still had it in me, **while knowing in my heart that it was no longer the work that I was meant to do,** *and no longer the work that fulfilled me and gave me* **authentic purpose in this life and in my "new normal,"** *I knew I needed* **more** *to make me want to* **get out of bed every day, and face the day...and a world without my husband, still* *in shock and emotionally traumatized by it all. Many things shifted within me the day he died...I was **broken open and broken down**, but through faith and the love and support of my friends and family, and most of all through the **gift of knowing with everything deep inside me, that I was being redirected by God** and that no matter what, He was taking Trent on that day, I **vowed to get stronger and serve my life's purpose by taking a leap of faith**, something I would have viewed before as a risk.*

*What I know for sure—is that as traumatic and devastating it was on that Friday, Nov. 2nd **when Trent came home to me to ultimately pass, that it was a gift**...After begging him not to go into work that morning and rest until the doctor's appointment I had made for him, he left anyway and returned home an hour later, to walk upstairs to our bedroom, place his hands at the foot of our bed and look at me...and then collapse to the floor where he gasped for breath as I struggled to hold him up and call 911. He took his last breath in the ambulance minutes later, unbeknown to me as I wouldn't let them stop working to resuscitate him for two hours later, insisting that this was not happening. A few days later, I was able to see early on, that **it was a gift that he came home to be with me to pass on from this life**...his Spirit on some level must have known. **It was a gift that his heart didn't stop beating while driving home, or earlier at work** even though he was working at the very hospital I would direct the ambulance to where they would* *pronounce him dead two hours later. I am able to have gratitude for his coming **home to be with me** and not have it happen earlier that morning in front of **Sophia as she kissed him goodbye for the last time before she got on the bus**, or the night before at the **last pre-game football dinner he would attend with Matt and Joe**. For this, I have gratitude and will **not be a Victim**, as I only know how to be a Victor. Not to mention he would have hated for me to spend more than the two months that I did sitting on the couch and in bed in disbelief not able to move or do much.*

I was "inspired by fitness" to get up and walk again, to get stronger and LIVE my new life, and to serve others through health and fitness. I have nothing but gratitude for the privilege of waking up at 5:30 a.m. during the week to prepare for my early morning clients and throughout the day as I lead my last client through stretching and our big "inhale the good, exhale any negative" breath, around 7 PM most nights. I am blown away with gratitude each and every snow day when clients still want to trek through the snow and ice to come to me to train and keep up on top of their improving health and fitness. I have immense gratitude for the transformations I see in my clients, the INTERNAL STRENGTH and confidence and the external strength as a result of our work on their overall health and fitness. I too am much stronger than I was a year ago—inside and out—yet I still work every day to get stronger and have to fight harder on some days. Although I can flip a tractor tire, jump tall boxes, perform headstands and pull ups and throw around heavy weights, I still can't reprogram the country music stations in my car and listen to country music…still working on getting the emotional strength for that one.

This January when I began to work on my 2014 Business Plan and create this year's vision board (a ritual I've done for 10 years now, even before the Book, The Secret made vision boards popular), I knew that last year was a year of survival and that my business began as self-prescribed grief therapy. This year, I would choose to step it up knowing that I'm serving my life's purpose, helping others live healthier, better lives and that is much more I can and am meant to do as I work to help others become INSPIRED BY FITNESS.

As I celebrate not just getting through the first year, but reflect on the 1-Year Anniversary of the privilege of serving others through INSPIRED BY FITNESS, I am grateful, humbled, honored, awakened, faithful and excited for what's ahead. Since the 1-Year in Business date crept up on me, I decided not to officially celebrate with my clients and supporters during this cold winter season, but look forward to celebrating this Spring where I plan to host an Open House in honor of those who have made it possible…One Bite At A Time, One Workout At A Time, One Healthy Choice At A Time and One Day At A Time! To each of you, I dedicate my favorite verse: "I can do all things through He who strengthens me" - Philippians 4:13

April 1, 2014

How can it be 18 months—an entire year and a half—since the morning Trent passed away...I find it unbelievable and still unreal that he isn't here and that it's been a year and a half since that day: November 2, 2012.

*Today my brother, Troy, and I were outside working on my yard. As he dug a path and laid cement pavers to create a walkway to our side door, a project Trent would have done, I noticed all of the debris in the mulch and yard leftover from last summer that I couldn't manage then. I realized I was starting to care again...care about the yard and taking better care of it. I didn't care so much last year and let projects like mulching, pulling weeds, cleaning up yard debris go by the wayside. Back then, I was doing all I could to just get through the days. On this April day, finally taking down the Christmas greenery in my front window boxes, I could see progress, **signs that I care and that I can do more than I could before.***

*I was talking to a girlfriend, as well as my brother and sister-in-law recently about how the 18 month anniversary was approaching and that it still feels like yesterday...I'm not sure what I've been doing all this time, yet I know I've **created a new normal that is much different than my "old life."** Somehow I've been able to launch a business that began as my grief therapy and has evolved into purposeful work that I get excited about when I get to rise early to serve others through health and fitness.*

*Although my heart is still broken and my body aches for and misses him, I'm choosing to be happy—**a new happy**...I'm grateful for my life and know that I am blessed. Grateful for the life we built and shared together, and excited for my future. I didn't think I would ever, ever be able to feel that way again.*

*I feel lucky that my Spirit is **alive**, has grown and evolved and that I know my power is on the inside and that Trent's Spirit is with me. It's our Internal Power that matters, not the external power—power that can be taken away from us, like material things, money, jobs, etc.* **Like the Good Witch Glenda said to Dorothy in the Wizard of Oz at the end, "My Dear, You've Always Had The Power Inside You, You Just Had To Learn It For Yourself." I'm glad I didn't have to wait to the end of my life to figure this out.**

*My grief journey moving forward has truly been one bite at a time. It's evolved from getting through one hour at a time to one day at a time. Everyone's grief is different. People often say "don't make any big changes for at least a year." But it would have been detrimental for me **not** to make big changes.*

*When you lose someone so close to you, it turns your world upside down and life as you knew it will never be the same again...the loss changes your entire life, a big change has **already** happened. I needed to **take a look at my life and purpose for being left behind.** I needed to make other big changes to help create a new normal and move forward.*

Everything about my life is different than before Trent died. My job, my family, my work hours, how I dress every day, what I care about and what I don't. **The people I spend time with are different**, *the true people or Spirits as I like to refer to them. The ones who have continued to show up, some unexpectedly, are the ones whose company I seek out and relish. I'm aware of those people who didn't show up, who haven't been there along the way and those who are still "waiting for me to get better" so I can be "normal" or fun to be around again or get back to helping them with their life, the way I used to.*

Part of my grief and the trauma of that morning is that I forget—A LOT. *Not just things, but events and people. Greif experts call this a result of being grief stricken and say the trauma from the event and loss impairs or erases memory. So, if I see you and forget how we know each other, or forget your name or a story or experience we shared together,* **please forgive me as I have lost some memory recall.**

What I know for sure is that **we are all Spirits having a human experience** *and that God and the Universe work together to support and love us, and that the gift of life is having gratitude for the experience and being true to ourselves.* **And that Spirit lives on…**

This is my Strength Rock. *This rock sits at the entrance of my neighborhood, about a mile from my house. When I first started to walk again and walk my old jogging path, I started to see the rock in a new way. In the beginning after Trent passed, just being able to walk to* my rock was an accomplishment. Being able to run again was **another accomplishment—or another "bite."** The rock started to inspire me to want to get stronger: to make it to the rock, then to perform pushups with my hands on its surface, and run back home, knowing I could do it again. When I reach the rock to do my routine of "rock pushups," I close my eyes and can hear the sounds of nature in a whole new way, as if the rock and I are one, standing strong, through the storms, surviving each season, and holding up against anything that comes our way, knowing we are part of the Universe, here to serve our purpose, though we are dented, weathered & cracked open, yet whole and solid.

When it came time to design the cover of this book, my strength rock kept appearing to me as the image that should be on the cover. Do you recognize it? She weathers the storms, not just surviving each season, but thriving, drawing in the light, standing strong as a symbol of strength and perseverance for anyone who is awake enough to notice.

January 29, 2015 This Thing Called Grief—My Awakening

I was having lunch with a friend this week who said they read my Blog about my grief journey. As part of my new normal, I've met a lot of wonderful people who are now in my life, mainly through my work and the people I am privileged to serve. I've also met new friends who didn't know Trent or me before, and I realized I haven't read any of the things I've written since I wrote them—part of my own therapy of writing and getting it all out and moving forward. **So it made me think, "what would someone who I didn't know until recently think & learn when they read my Grief Blogs?"** I know at the core I'm the same person, but I'm also different in a lot of ways—**a result of the Shift and now aware that the place I am now I can only describe as being "Awakened."** What I also know is being cracked open and brought to my knees is part of the **Shift** I've experienced

I figured I was pretty raw and open when I wrote and knew it had been a while since my last written reflection, since Trent's birthday in October. Getting through the **holidays this past year, my coping mechanism was to make myself super busy and suppress**. It worked pretty well since I didn't cry on our Wedding Anniversary, his 2 year passing date, Thanksgiving or Christmas and I made sure I was surrounded by family and friends to create new, happy memories and traditions. That doesn't mean I didn't cry in between, but it's becoming less and less and more far and few between instead of a regular occurrence as it used to be. The grief still hits me and affects me by occasional extreme fatigue and that's when I know I better acknowledge it and get it out. And, I still can't remember things, events or people, especially the first year after his passing.

So, I re-read all of my Grief Blogs the other night. Wow, not only do I barely remember writing any of it, but I wondered how could I have expressed all of that? When I re-read each one, it sounds like I was doing pretty well, and able to be very open and share, which is something I don't typically do unless it's within my close circle. So I was surprised when I read some of the things I shared. Showing vulnerability or asking for help has never been my thing. So reading my Grief Journey made me feel pretty vulnerable and for the first time, totally ok with that. Especially when I saw posts from people that I had not seen before and was overwhelmed with their support, love and encouragement. I then thought that maybe I should write an update since some people seem to really care and want to know how this journey is going.

As life would have it, the very next morning (yesterday), I got a FaceBook message from my friend Heather, who I haven't seen in a long time, who said she had read my grief Journey the night before and that she was "so glad I blog so she can keep up on how I am." She shared she lost her mom unexpectedly last September and the difficulties she's experienced, and that "your words help and really hit home and helped and that I am so many things to so many people and that I continue to inspire in ways I don't realize." Again, wow moment and overcome with love, support (and still humbly surprised when people tell me this) and that YES, I need to keep writing and sharing my story and grief journey so that other people can be helped. Of course, each in their own way.

Feb. 2nd will mark the 2 year, 3 month anniversary of Trent's sudden passing. What I know for sure is that this thing called the **Grief Journey is constant and doesn't have a deadline or timeframe**, even though some people would like there to be. Those of us going through the grief process know we are different. Those around us usually can't fully understand why we (survivors) are so different or how every day activities, months or years later, can trigger the pain of our loss. As one of my new friends, Michelle, who happens to be a widow herself shared with me last week, it can be something as simple as fixing a particular meal for her kids, knowing her husband would have loved it. And then all of the sudden, make her feel like she's been kicked in the gut, knocking her back down to her knees. I SOOO got that, as I have moments where *out of nowhere, things are flowing well and happily then something will trigger me unexpectedly to feel ripped open & torn apart. And those that think, "Still? She still feels like that?" YES, still and it's okay…whether you understand or not.*

What I know for sure is that I now have more good days than bad days. I still choose to be happy and am really enjoying the continued creation of my new normal. I love my new life and I know how blessed I am and I am excited for what the future will bring. I wake up each morning with immense gratitude and excitement for what the day brings and what I want to accomplish. My morning ritual starts with prayer of gratitude (along with my lemon water) and a brief (I'm talking 2 minutes or so) meditation, something I'm really trying to practice! I didn't think I could ever get to this place, not even a year ago. I know that I am connected to the other side and I'm fully aware that I am being guided. I also know I'm serving my Divine Purpose—to serve others by helping people live their best lives through health and fitness.

What I know for sure is that I have been **Awakened** *and that I have become* **aware again***, and am open and always seeking to learn more. When I made my vision board for 2015, as I've done for 11 years, I chose the title theme* **"Lighter, Brighter & Energized"***. That sums up where I am today and what I want to create more of—to be for others and myself. And I still take it* **One Bite At A Time, One Day At A Time***.*

If you're reading this, thank you. **Thank you** *for your encouragement, support and inspiration. Love, Susan*

P.S. This photo was taken at the Indianapolis Zoo, when I took Sophia, my nephew Jeff and neighbor kids Megan and Jack to the Zoo. It was the first time I had been since before Trent passed and a "full circle" moment where I got to meet in person, Sophie The Elephant, who is a significant part of my story, grief journey and my Awakening.

May 28, 2015 What it means to turn age 46

Today, I was lucky enough to turn age 46, a milestone birthday. Although it's not a typical milestone, it's one that I've been thinking about for over two years. ***I usually say that "age is just a number," but this age is one that I am happy and grateful to celebrate with mixed emotions.*** *Because Trent died just 3 weeks after his 46th birthday, I am first just hoping to make it past 46 & 3 weeks, and I want to honor this age and this year in every way. As the Tim McGraw song says, I want to "live like I were dying" because life can change in an instant.*

When I woke up to the brightness of the beautiful day coming through my window and the birds chirping I laid in bed for a moment and thanked God and the Universe for waking up to a new day, for Sophia asleep in her room and for my parents still being here, for the sunshine (thankful it wasn't rainy or gloomy) and being able to live to see another birthday, and for feeling healthy and stronger than I have been these past two weeks. ***I haven't felt my best the past couple of weeks as I have found happens when faced with a "Trent date," such as his birthday, our anniversary, his passing date or any holiday.***

Grief for me, shows up in the form of fatigue and slight neck and back pain. ***This is what happens when you suppress emotions in order to get through—our body responds and has to process it somehow so physical pain can show up as a direct result of emotional pain or stress!*** *I've found that the days leading up to a Trent date are often harder than the actual day itself, and it's a relief the next day to get through and past it.*

My birthdays in general have been really hard without him here. We always made a big deal out of birthdays, partly because we liked to celebrate everything but also because we always talked about how grateful we were for one another and for another birthday since some people didn't make it to our age.

So, I had a brief moment this morning when I woke up, after I said thanks and noticed I felt better, and then looked at **the empty space next to me in bed, still in somewhat disbelief that he really isn't here. A brief pause, that could have easily kept me in bed,** but the shift that continues within me and the feeling of knowing his Spirit is with me and that God and the Universe are guiding me got me up and excited for what the day would bring. **When I sipped my first cup of coffee, I said out loud, "Bring it On 46!"**

It's been a really good birthday. I am overwhelmed with all of the love that surrounded me throughout the day with each & every person who reached out through phone calls, emails, texts, flowers sent, Facebook, Instagram & LinkedIn birthday posts, cards and gifts. **I know that God sends love through people and I also know that our Light shines brightest when we give and receive Love.** My Light is able to shine because of the many wonderful people in my life—long time friends and family, clients and new friends who I know God has brought into my life to help create my new normal.

What it means to turn 46 is that I GOT TO celebrate another birthday...that I am lighter and more *grateful, that I want to have more fun and step it up professionally and personally in my life, that I'm finally ready to listen to Country music again, that I'm stronger, wiser and better than I was at 45 because I continue to work on myself, to seek and grow Spiritually and strive to bring Light & Love to those I am with and to situations I am tested with.* **What it means to get to live another day is that we still have work to do, lessons to learn, people to serve and uplift and a life to LIVE!**

November 2, 2015

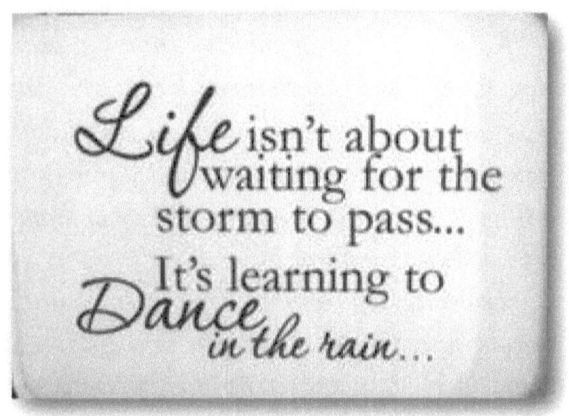

I realized recently, that I find myself referring to most events, and my life, separated into two phases - "Before Trent passed and After Trent Passed." As I observe the 3-year anniversary today of Trent's sudden passing, a gamut of emotions run through my mind, and my heart. First the obvious of, how on earth can it be 3 years??? Pardon my French, but WTF!

There are 3 things - or lessons - in 3 Years I've learned. I hope by sharing it helps you or someone you know in some way:

1. ***What I know for sure is that grief is an ongoing, evolving, very personal and unpredictable emotion and experience.*** *It's a process with no end and no deadline, although some people may want or expect you to have an end with your grief, and your tough days, and "get on with your life, already!" Usually so* **they** *can feel more comfortable.*

    We will all experience loss at some point. It's a part of life. Levels of loss are subjective and until you've experienced the loss of someone you loved, unconditionally, more than anything and more than you could have ever imagined loving someone and that you never fathomed losing, it's difficult to understand or to know what to do when someone you know is suffering a loss. ***Until you've been cracked open, broken down and brought to your knees by grief, tragedy or whatever life challenge knocks you down, it's hard to understand.*** *I get that now.*

2. ***And I've learned over these three years not to take it personally or be upset when someone says something that sounds utterly ridiculous, insensitive or offensive, such as*** *"Are you still going to stay in that house?" or "Don't you think you should be dating by now, because he probably would". Until recently, these types of comments or questions would be very upsetting,*

now it makes me laugh when I retell it to a girlfriend. Still a bit off-putting, but I know most people mean well, it's just they just don't understand. I've grown and evolved to a place of peace with this and to not get upset with people who don't understand and still want me to be the "old Susan", you know, before Trent passed. **It's kind of like the judgments we make toward parents on how to parent their children when we're not a parent ourselves and then we become a parent and all of the "I'd never let my kid do that or I would never raise my children that way" goes out the window!** *Until you experience it, you really don't get it. It changes everything and we're never the same. But hopefully we choose to become better than we were before. To be a Victor and not a Victim of our circumstance, whether loss, tragedy or whatever circumstance - fill in the blank.*

I got through the entire month of October - his birthday and our wedding anniversary - without any tears. That is until this morning. I started this morning getting Sophia ready for school and out the door focusing on the positive and reminding her that **"Life isn't about waiting for the storm to pass.....It's learning to Dance in the rain...." and that this is what we would do today,** *just as Trent would want us to. And just as this plaque in our kitchen (pictured above) from Trent's sister, Tracie and my brother-in-law Ron, brought us on a surprise visit in December after Trent died, reminds us. I then practiced Day 1 of the Deepak Chopra 21-Day Meditation Experience and centered* *with today's meditation mantra **"My Beliefs Enhance My Life".** After a few text messages from friends and family, one in particular made my cry for just a few seconds before I declared my mantra and stopped..........I believe this with every fiber of my being. And, if you know me or work with me at Inspired By Fitness, you know how much I believe in positive affirmations and the power of faith, love and light.*

3. **What I know for sure is that I have been able to create a new healthy, happy normal because of my beliefs that there is more good to come and that choosing love and light over fear and darkness brings more light and love** *in every area of our life and for those around us. I'm a work in progress................doing my best to embrace the process of grief, dance in the rain and live my best life through serving others through health, fitness and love. I have immense gratitude for my life and all its lessons. I love my life and the new normal I've created.* **My story continues to evolve and I hope sharing it helps others find their own strength to move forward and find their internal power. To choose love and light over fear and darkness, even when (fill in the blank). To discover their purpose and take a leap of faith to pursue it.**

One Bite At A Time, One Day At A Time.

With gratitude and love, Susan

This was my last blog post about my grief journey. It's been a while since I felt compelled to share through my blog and a lot has happened since. Perhaps because in writing this book, my journey has unfolded with each page and with each revelation. I've shared events and details about my life and the lessons learned that I've not shared with some of those who are closest to me and it's been a helpful reminder that through shared suffering, we can heal ourselves and others, as we grow and transform and embrace the process. One bite at a time.

I've learned a lot about grief and suffering, and what to do when someone I know loses someone. It boils down to one simple thing. Showing up. Again and again. Showing up and not having to say a word, but just being there. I've also learned what not to do or say when someone I know is suffering or loses someone.

Top 10 Things Not To Say When Someone Is Grieving, Specifically The Loss of A Spouse
(Things people have really said to me)

1. "Are you going to stay in the house? I could never stay there."

This is an unnecessary, judgmental and heart wrenching question to ask someone who just lost a spouse. Especially if the question is followed with stating what you would or couldn't do. Or how hard it would be to stay in the house. Because what you're really expressing to a widow/widower is your opinion on what you think they should do or what you would do, when you really can't comprehend until you're in that situation.

For me, my home gave me comfort and became my refuge. My safe place. Being in my house made me feel closer to Trent. Even though I could see him everywhere and every corner of every room held a memory, it brought me peace and made me feel more connected. Even in our bedroom, where he collapsed at the foot of our bed. I felt like he was with me. Still today, almost four years later, I can still feel his presence in our house. I see him around the house in memories or in the image of his Spirit and it brings me peace, and a mix of sadness and happiness. But that's part of the process and part of the journey.

2. "Everything happens for a reason."

This is one of the worst things to say to someone after a loss because there is no reason that the death of a loved one can help someone feel better. Unless due to elderly age, there is no good reason to take the pain away or explain the loss of a spouse, child, parent, sibling or loved one. There are simply some things we can't explain or understand. Things that just suck and are shitty to go through. Period. Things we can only grow to accept in order to heal and go on. Loss is one of them. There doesn't need to be a reason. This goes back to just showing up and not worrying about what to say or how to try to explain the loss away. What's important is how we view the reason we're still here. And the work we're here to do. Death is a part of life. We're all going to die. Death gives us a really good reason to look at our own life and re-evaluate who we want to be and how we want to live moving forward.

3. "Are you dating yet? Well if he was here, he'd be dating by now." Or "Do you think he'd be dating by now?"

WTF? This is a loaded, please don't even go there question. I was amazed at how often I was asked this after the first year and it's the number one question I get asked today. Early on, I felt insulted, offended and devastated at the idea of the question. Asking this can be received as not only offensive and hurtful if someone's not ready to even think about dating again, but also as pure nosiness. And I highly recommend not following it up with an opinion that the other person would be dating by now if they were here instead. Ouch. Tacky and doubly inappropriate.

4. "Don't you think it's about time you moved on?"

You mean because I'm not dating anyone yet or fill in the blank of what's really behind this question? Even though I've moved on in everything else in my life and moved on through each day, I'm not moving on in your eyes because I'm not dating anyone yet? I wanted to scream this at times! There is no timeline for moving on in any aspect of grief, especially dating again. Figuring out your new normal and moving through it is a process. Taking each day, moment, anniversary, holiday, social situation and event one bite at a time is moving on. Creating our new reality once we wake up from the fog—or the nightmare—is moving on. Transforming out of the darkness and into the light is moving on. Moving on may not look like what you think it should for someone else. So move on to a different question. Or don't ask any questions. Just show up and be there.

5. "What's wrong, you're still sad?"

Really? Still sad? Hell yes I'm still sad! It was about a year and a half after Trent passed and I was at a nail salon getting my nails done. I'd left my sunroof open overnight and it had rained. My car was filled with water and I was faced with another moment of not having my husband there to help or pick me up at the car detail shop while they cleaned my car. I was on my own and felt very alone. It was one of those "straw that broke the camel's back" moments of going through the motions to get through the days, thinking you're doing well and then comes along something that just knocks you back down to your knees. Reminding you that with all the time that has passed and all the good days, there will still be bad days and moments that hit you out of nowhere. It's part of the process.

For me, part of that process was learning to ask for help. The lesson was learning that when we allow ourselves to be vulnerable and *ask* for help, it can not only make us stronger, it helps give others a way to help us, when they didn't know how to before. Part of my angst was that as a single mom again and no drivers in the house, I had no one to help me with things like dropping off my car and needing a ride. So I called my friend Beth who had continued to show up for me, assuring me she was there if and when I needed anything. She later told me how much it meant to her that I reached out to her for help. And that it made her feel like she was able to finally do something to help with what I was going through. It was an aha moment for me to realize that by accepting help, I was helping someone else.

Because of the car ordeal, I'd had a rough, emotional morning missing Trent and wasn't able to hold back my tears throughout my appointment. My nail lady who I'd been going to for four years and who knew Trent couldn't understand why tears were running down my face. When I told her I was having a rough morning because of Trent, she looked puzzled and asked why and if I was still sad about Trent. As if I shouldn't still be sad. As if I should be over losing my husband. After being crushed by this question, I got pissed for a couple of minutes at her insensitivity and lack of emotional intelligence. My irritation soon turned to pity for her, knowing she must not have ever loved or been loved the way I had. I knew she couldn't possibly understand the grief journey of a real, true love lost. So I became sad for her, instead of myself. I transformed the way I reacted and moved on.

Grief has no deadlines. It never ends, it just changes. By asking someone if they're still sad over their loss regardless of how much time has passed, is like asking if they still love or remember their loved one. For me, I now have less frequent sad days, but I still have sad moments, even in the midst of my joy and my happy days.

    6. "I know how you feel. I felt like that after my divorce."

Let me preface this by saying I understand first hand that going through a divorce is a loss. Through divorce, we grieve the loss of a marriage and a life we once had. But let me assure you, divorce doesn't compare to losing a spouse, a marriage, a family and a life you once had as a result of death. I've experienced the darkness, the wounds and the heartache of both. And I've rebounded from and been transformed by both. The journeys can be similar, but the death of a spouse is not the same as the death of a marriage. Even if you aren't the one who initiated your divorce, don't compare your divorce to someone who's spouse just died. A divorce is a formal breakup, an end of relationship and a loss of a marriage. A death is the loss of a life. Make sense?

    7. "How long are you going to wear your wedding ring?" Or, "You're still wearing your wedding ring (in that disapproving, judgmental tone)? or "I noticed you took off your wedding ring. Does that mean you're dating?"

Unlike a divorce, there is no deadline (as in when the divorce is final) or timeframe to how long to continue wearing your wedding ring after the death of a spouse. Some widows/widowers, especially when older, wear their wedding ring until the day they die. For me, the moment came unexpectedly when the pain of wearing my ring became more than taking it off.

Because I use my hands a lot in my work and when I talk, I would often knick my ring on things. I don't remember exactly how long into the second year it was, but one day when I was on the treadmill running, my hand swung and hit the handle bar, causing me to stop and make sure I didn't knock out the diamond. It was in that jolting moment that I had enough. Enough of the pain of looking at it every day, no longer giving me comfort, just more pain. That was it for me. It wasn't some big decision or deadline I'd made to stop wearing it. It simply became more painful than comforting to wear it.

For some it can be an emotional, thought out decision to stop wearing their wedding ring. For others, it can simply be that it doesn't serve them anymore. And for some it really is because they are open to and ready to date again. The reason doesn't matter. It's a personal choice and one that shouldn't be questioned by anyone else.

8. "You wear his ashes in that heart necklace around your neck? That's creepy."

What brings comfort to us may be uncomfortable for others. Because we all grieve differently and are evolved differently as people and spiritual beings with different beliefs, where and how we seek to stay connected to our lost loved one will differ greatly. Learn to accept how those you seek to comfort are coping. You may not understand it and that's okay. Whatever you may find odd, weird or creepy may be exactly the thing you'll say you'll never do, but will find yourself doing and understanding when you too, lose someone you love. It's part of the grieving process. Your role is to just show up with a "no judge, just love" bundle of support.

Per Trent's wishes, he was cremated. We used to laugh and joke about the scene from the movie *Meet The Parents*, when Ben Stiller knocks over the urn on Robert De Niro's fireplace. Trent would crack up and we'd talk about how when we were older and passed on, we wanted to be cremated. He said that if I died first he was going to drink my ashes so I would always be a part of him. I would then tell him how he couldn't do that beause he would have to pass me out!

When Trent passed, I had an urn heart necklace made for myself and one for Trent's mom. I also had custom football Dad angel urns made for both Matt and Joe and a heart urn for Sophia. And I had a backup heart urn made for myself as well, thanks to my friend Jacqueline who said it would be a good idea in case I lost my necklace. I would have never thought of getting a backup urn. It seemed so critical at the time, so I did. Little did I know I would receive a call a year and a half later from the funeral home asking when I planned to pick up the rest of Trent's ashes. What? I wasn't aware there were any remaining ashes after the mortuary guy delivered the urns to our house shortly after the Celebration of Life Service.

When I arrived to pick up the ashes, I was presented with a white box that felt like it weighed thirty pounds. I wasn't sure what to expect, but I certainly didn't expect there would be that many left over ashes and that it would weigh so much. So I drove home with the heavy box and laughed to myself as I walked in our family room, facing our own fireplace and talked to Trent about what to do with him. I knew he didn't want to be placed on the fireplace. So I did what anyone would do with leftover "inventory" and stored it in a cabinet for replacement urns in the future.

I wore my heart urn necklace every day for about two years, giving me comfort having a part of him with me at all times. I still wear it when I feel the need or desire to. The only reason I quit wearing it every day is because one day during a workout that involved Burpees, my necklace banged my tooth, which provided another comic relief moment. After explaining to Trent (yes, I'm aware he didn't talk back, but I'm a big believer in continuing to talk to our lost loved ones knowing that they are listening and guiding us) that I had to stop wearing the necklace because I couldn't have him chipping my tooth, so I took it off. Not because my grieving was over as some assumed, but because I was honestly worried I'd chip my tooth. Even though I know ashes are just part of the physical body and that Spirit lives on, it comforted me and made me feel closer to him.

One evening when I was out with some friends and was asked about my urn necklace, someone in the group said, "Ewe, you wear his ashes around your neck? That's creepy." This happened to be one of Trent's closest friends and I knew he didn't mean anything by it and that he wasn't as spiritually connected, so it didn't upset me too much because I love and understand him. In fact, I could almost hear Trent laughing at his good buddy's comment, just as he would have laughed with him if he were there with us, so I actually got a kick out of it. But it did get me wondering how many other people thought it was weird and creepy. Part of my shift and transformation allowed me to giggle to myself knowing that people thought it was crazy, and that was perfectly okay.

I share this example with you so that when and if you find something weird or creepy that someone else does to remember, honor or grieve their loved one, seek to understand first so that you may grow and learn from it. You may not understand it and that's okay. Just don't voice it out loud in case the person isn't as evolved and understanding of *your* lack of understanding. Sophia wears Trent's t-shirts to bed almost every night, and sometimes I do too. It comforts us to do so still, almost four years later. Some people wonder when we'll stop. We may never stop seeking comfort in wearing his oversized t-shirts, and that's okay.

9. "I'm sorry I haven't called or been around, it's been really hard for me."

Even if you are also grieving the loss of your friend or family member's loss, please do not tell them you haven't shown up for them because it's been hard on you. This makes it all about you and can be received as being selfish and inconsiderate of your friend or family's feelings and needs. Because what they need is you. You to show up and grieve and remember with them. Not distance yourself or desert them during their suffering. No matter how difficult the loss or suffering is for you too.

10. "I left you a message but I never heard back."

Expect not to hear back from someone who calls, texts or emails after the death of their loved one. This is a good time to practice letting go of your ego and practice compassion and understanding. So if you're offended or rationalizing in your head that you reached out once but are waiting until you hear back, look at this as a time to transform your maturity level, emotional intelligence and spiritual growth.

Not only is it likely that they are overwhelmed with people reaching out, but they probably aren't in an emotional state to talk or return your call promptly, if ever. This goes back to reaching out and showing up again and again, even if you don't get a response. If you really want to know what to do for your friend or family member who's grieving, this is the number one thing to do—show up and keep showing up. Don't worry about what to say or saying anything at all. Just keep reaching out to express your support, thoughts and prayers and physically show up to just be there, by their side.

How to comfort when someone has lost a parent.

Brene' Brown brilliantly shares in her book, *Daring Greatly* her parent manifesto, which says "Together we will cry and face fear and grief. I will want to take away your pain but instead will sit with you and teach you how to feel it." This sums up what I've learned about how to comfort a child (or an adult) who has experienced a loss, illness or any suffering.

As a parent, one of the greatest gifts we can offer our children is to teach them how to feel their pain and transform their suffering so they won't transmit it in unhealthy ways, but help lead them through so they may rise up from it.

Unless a child has friends who have also lost a parent, their friends can't possibly understand the grief your child is and will be experiencing. Their friends will quickly go on with their lives, not understanding that months or years later, the grief and pain continues with each missed birthday, holiday, milestone or random trigger. And this will add another layer to the grief that a child will experience when they lose a parent. Helping them understand that their friends can't fully understand until they one day experience the loss of their own parent, can help teach them how to manage their feelings of isolation, resentment and pain. And to help them feel it, express it and not feel as alone.

In addition to my kids, I have many adult friends who have lost either their mom or dad or both. As a result of learning from my own grief journey, one thing I now do on Mother's Day and Father's Day (as well as the parent's birthday or death anniversary date if I know it), is to send a text to all of my friends who've lost a parent to let them know I'm thinking of them on Mother's Day or Father's Day. It's just a simple, brief text, but it's genuine and sent with love and intended to comfort and remember with my friends their lost parent, no matter how long it's been since they passed on. It's my way of showing up, knowing that the little things matter. And that to acknowledge and remember a lost parent, even 20 years later, means a lot, as the grief of a loss never ends.

I find each year that this group text on Father's Day and Mother's Day grows and my heart aches for my friends on those days. As I celebrate and give thanks for my own mom and dad who are ages 80 and 75, I seek how to show up for those who have lost theirs.

Top 5 Grief Myths Debunked

1. Time heals all wounds.

Time does not heal all wounds. Time passing, just like our loved one's passing, doesn't cure, put an end to or permanently heal us. Time can either make it easier or harder on some days. The wound is always open and susceptible to scabs known as special dates, anniversaries, holidays, memories, vacations, a milestone in our own life without our loved one here to share it or simply a random trigger in the form of a bad day.

A daughter won't be any less sad on her wedding day without her father to walk her down the aisle twenty years later or two years later. A parent's wound of losing their child will be opened again each birthday, anniversary of the death date, graduation or other events of their child's friends and other memorable dates and future moments without their child here to share it with.

For a widow or widower, time won't heal the emptiness and feelings of being left out of couples dinners, social events or friend's gatherings. Or not wanting to attend certain social events solo, as it can make us feel our loss even more. Time doesn't heal the sadness or pit in the stomach on wedding anniversaries, holidays or filling out a form and having to check the dreaded widow box.

Time passing, like grief, is also a process that changes. It can make it easier and it can make it harder. I've found that the more time passes, the more other people forget. And that makes it harder. Yet, as time passes, my bad days are fewer and my new normal seems like it's been this way for longer than it has been, making it easier, yet harder to believe my husband's been gone for almost four years. Making me sad and in disbelief, yet still happy and at peace with my new life, grateful for the time we had. Time changes and can lessen the pain of the wound, but it doesn't permanently heal.

What helps us heal is feeling everything we feel and not denying our grief. As Dr. Christiane Northrup says, "We must feel it to heal it." And if we don't feel our grief and allow ourselves to be sad, angry, and all of the mixed emotions that come along and change day after day, it will fester within us and come out as toxic, unhealthy behavior or physical illness. And this is what keeps us from healing.

Time spent going through the motions, getting through the days, months and years can help us along our grief journey, but unless we are acknowledging our grief, expressing and getting it out, seeking to be better as a result and not remaining a victim, but becoming a victor in our own life, our wounds cannot heal. There is no way around it. Not even waiting for time to pass. We must move *through* it and embrace the process. Tears, heartache, loneliness, all the sucky (Yes, I'm making that a word because it sucks sometimes, no matter how much time passes) parts and all. We must feel it all to help in our healing. And then we keep moving forward, transforming out of the darkness and into the light. Blooming from the wound where time stopped and you once bled. One bite at a time.

2. Don't make any big decisions for at least a year.

My experience with grief has taught me the opposite of what I've always heard about loss and what many people told me after Trent passed. When your loved one dies, especially your spouse, you're immediately faced with countless big decisions. To wait for an entire year to address some of the things that need taken care of and not make any decisions is not only counterproductive but would be a form of denial and postponing a big part of the grief process. At least it felt like that for me. Losing my husband was the biggest and worst thing I've ever experienced. To not make any big decisions or changes for a year would have prevented me from feeling all the crap I had to deal with, thus not contributing to the healing process. To leave everything else the same when the biggest piece was missing would have made it harder and been detrimental.

 I can't imagine waiting a year to decide what to do with Trent's rig, as he liked to refer to his Ford Expedition. Knowing that neither of the boys wanted or needed his oversized SUV and feeling sick to my stomach when I would look out in the driveway or pull onto our street and see his car in our driveway, I knew I had to "move on" and sell his car. When asked if I planned to stay in our house, I knew immediately I wasn't going anywhere and made a big decision to stay in the house. I made many other big decisions and changes that saved me from staying in the darkness of grief. I quit my job and started my own business as part of my self-prescribed grief therapy. I donated most of my business suits and items in our storage unit, downsizing to a smaller, more affordable one. I donated most of my clothing that reminded me of Trent. Outfits that when I looked at them, recalled the memory of wearing it with Trent. I also donated Trent's business suits and clothing that the boys didn't want or could never grow into to a charity that helped men get back on their feet, as I knew Trent would have wanted. I had to change how I felt when I walked in our closet so I wouldn't fall to my knees again, in pure anguish, sobbing and hiding from the outside world, not facing the reality that he was gone. The pain of not making any changes and keeping these "things" became worse than the pain of making the decisions and moving forward. I was forced to make decisions, small and big. So I did. One bite at a time.

Everyone will handle making decisions differently. But what I want you to know is that it's not just okay, it is very healing and healthy to make big and small decisions the first year as part of the grief process. Do what makes *you* feel better, regardless of when or how much time as passed.

3. You'll get back to "normal" once you get back to your old routine

I heard this one a lot in the beginning. Nothing will feel normal at first. We have to create a new normal and sometimes a whole new routine just to feel a sense of normalcy. Creating a new normal is part of the process of making changes and big decisions the first year. We can't just go back to our same old routine as if nothing has happened. Doing so can be detrimental to our healing by denying nothing has changed, denying our emotions. We can't just go back and expect to make a comeback. In order to experience an awakening and begin to transform out of the darkness and into the light, we must create a new normal, a new routine and a new positive reality. One change, one new routine, one new normal, one bite at a time.

4. The first year is the worst.

The first year sucks, but it's not always the worst. This is a big myth. The first year is a blur. The worst is when you wake up and come out of the fog, out of denial and face your new reality. The worst is when everyone else's life goes on normally and you're still reeling from the pain of your loss, figuring out your new normal. The worst is when it's three years later and you still have a hard time breathing when you relive the moment your loved one died. The worst is when others think you should be over it and don't understand why you do or don't want to do what helps you cope and move forward in your new positive reality. The worst is years later when all is going well and then out of nowhere, something happens and the sting of your loss knocks you down again. The worst is when it feels like everyone around you has forgotten, and the wound of your loss is still open, unaffected by time.

If you're grieving a loss and wondering if it's "normal" to feel the way you feel after the first year, or why it feels worse now in some ways than it did in the first year, know that it's perfectly normal to feel worst after the first year. And if you know someone who has suffered a loss and it's been longer than a year, don't assume it's any better or easier for them. The grief process continues long after the first year. Show up by reaching out to them and let them know you're thinking of them and remembering their loved one.

Every now and then I'll get a text from one of Trent's best friends, Jason, sharing a joke or something funny that reminds him of Trent. Jason is known as a jokester and not someone who is as emotionally expressive. Yet he's one of only a couple of Trent's friends that still reaches out on a regular basis to share a memory and send a funny text that we both know would have made Trent laugh. It's his way of showing up and remembering, when so many others have forgotten or stopped reaching out.

5. You'll never be happy again.

I thought I could never be happy again. I remember saying after Trent passed that I'd never be able to be happy again. I couldn't fathom it at the time. What I know for sure is that when we experience a loss, we're never the same, but eventually you'll feel happiness as long as you choose to do so. This is the difference maker—choosing to be happy, even when…because happiness is a choice. We must choose to show up in our own life and choose what to do and how to be better as a result of our loss. Choosing to be happy, doesn't take away from your grief or pain and doesn't mean you're over it. It means honoring your lost loved one and your own life by choosing to be happy, just as they would want. It means letting go of any guilt for finding happiness again.

I talked about earlier how the first tragedy is losing a loved one and that the second tragedy would be to not go on living our own life as best we can. It may take a while to feel happiness or to choose happiness, but ultimately it's a choice. You can and you will be happy again, even in the midst of your grief and even though your heart still aches for you lost loved one, you can be happy again. And it's not just okay, it's a tragedy not to.

As part of my transformation, I find happiness in so many more little things than I did before my husband passed. Because I'm more present in my life and have slowed down to be more present with others and outdoors in nature, I find happiness by taking things one bite at a time. I appreciate more, love more, forgive and accept more which creates more happiness.

As a result of slowing down and being more present, one of the silver linings of my grief and transformational shift is that I can now take naps! I used to view napping as a luxury that I could never relax my mind enough to experience. I even resented Trent at times because he could fall asleep within seconds for short naps and I couldn't, as my mind was too busy thinking about everything I thought I needed to do as I longed for a twenty minute nap. Now that my mind is more settled, relaxed and at peace I'm able to embrace the power of a power nap. Thanks to Arianna Huffington, founder of The Huffington Post and author of one of my favorite books, *Thrive* I'm also able to nap guilt-free. I share the teachings of her third metric to redefining success and creating a life of well-being, wisdom and wonder in my coaching business with my private and corporate clients, two of which have implemented a Relaxation Room for their employees at their companies as a result. Arianna teaches us the power and importance of valuing rest, napping and getting seven to nine hours of sleep each night, something our culture has undervalued. In *Thrive*, she helps us redefine what it means to be successful, and gives us not only permission, but advocates for us to reconnect with ourselves, our loved ones and our community by practicing healthy habits such as more sleep and naps so that we may thrive.

Along with my spiritual practices of positive affirmations, prayers and meditation, seeking to learn more and BE better, there is still a part of the old me that sometimes drops the F-bomb. Making me very happy at the time. Maybe it's the Gemini in me who has both sides of expression and both ends of the spectrum in me. Perhaps I like a healthy blend of yin and yang. For as much as I lean toward and am inspired by the gentle, loving teachings of Louise Hay, Marianne Williamson and Gabby Bernstein, I'm right there with Cheryl Strayed when I say GRIEVE like a motherfucker. CHOOSE HAPPINESS like a motherfucker and SHOW UP like a motherfucker!

Showing Up IS the most important thing we can do for someone who loses a loved one. And then, continue showing up, even and especially after the first year. I believe God sends us love through people. The number of people who showed up, sent letters, cards, and messages took my breath away. I remember going to the mailbox during the first couple of months and feeling an overwhelming sense of love and support by the huge stacks of cards and letters from people from all walks of our life. Not just from those I knew, but from people I'd never met and a few I didn't think even really cared for me all that much. I remember crying in disbelief, touched by each and every word. It would sometimes take an hour just to read each of the daily cards and letters. The love that was sent each day after Trent passed helped me endure the sadness and reaffirmed my faith in the darkness.

We're taught that love never ends in the words of one of the most cited love definitions, Corinthians Chapter 1 Verse 13—"Love bears all things, hopes all things, endures all things. Love never ends." It's our deep love for those we've lost that not just results in enduring the immense pain and suffering of losing them, but it can help us endure life after they are gone when we truly believe that the love never ends. The suffering we endure can transform the way we bear and endure life afterwards.

And when we go on in our new normal and *choose* to create a new positive reality of a new life without our loved one here by our side, we can then honor and keep that love alive. Choosing to be happy in your new normal doesn't take away from the love for your lost loved one, it actually honors them and allows you to transform your own life. So remember to own and embrace your story and your journey, whether you're moving through the loss of a loved one or the loss of your health, a job or any type of loss.

CHAPTER 5

Lesson: Be Awakened By Animals

"An animal's eyes have the power to speak a great language."

—Martin Buber

Elephants, Deer, Dogs and Birds, Oh My

A few weeks after Trent passed, sometime in late November, I felt the urge to leave the house by myself for the first time, to go on a walk. The walls in my house were closing in on me and I felt like I was fighting off a breakdown. It was cold, and I normally wouldn't have walked in the cold air, but this was one of the new things I didn't care about. Being cold didn't bother me then the way it used to. So I bundled up and ventured out my front door with my head down, and Rudy by my side, not wanting to see anyone or be seen. I still couldn't talk without crying and I just needed to move and regroup. Step by step, I forged ahead, head down, numb to the cold, and not wanting to believe it was all real. About a mile in, Rudy pulled on his leash to the side as a squirrel crossed by. Too weak to restrain him, I stopped and looked up as a warmth came over me and met the gaze of a deer, a buck about fifteen feet away, staring deep into my eyes. It wasn't a deer-caught-in-the-headlights kind of stare. It was a full on, intense stare down for what seemed like a full minute. I felt with everything in me that it was Trent showing up in the form of a deer as if to tell me he was there, watching me, comforting me with his warmth and sending the message through the presence and gaze of the deer, that all would be well. I felt an overwhelming sense of peace and warmth, as the deer slowly started to walk away, disappearing into the woods. This animal's eyes had the power to speak a great language. His eyes said it all and from that moment on, I knew Trent would always be with me. I also knew I needed to start looking up and paying attention to how the budding life of nature was all around me, supporting me, and soothing my soul.

If it weren't for Rudy being distracted by the squirrel, I would have missed my deer encounter—this was a lesson to look up and move forward. As we continued walking, I felt a sudden energy and joy as I embraced and reveled in the moment, laughing out loud at the thought of it all. Trent wouldn't come for a visit as a bird or a butterfly, he would come as a big, strong buck! I knew with everything in me what had just happened. I also knew when I told people, they would think I was crazy, which made me even giddier. Those few that would believe would also be amazed as they too knew it was just like Trent to appear in the animal form that he did.

Today when I walk that same path as I do almost weekly in the warmer months, my eyes are always open, seeking the beauty in nature, looking ahead and up at the trees, secretly hoping to one day see my deer again. Yet I know my magical encounter was a gift that keeps giving, not necessary to be seen again. I had learned the lesson, so it doesn't need to be repeated again.

You Say He's Just a Dog?

We added Rudy to our newly blended family a few months after we married. Trent had trained hunting dogs and researched top-of-the-line Labrador breeders on his quest to find the best dog for our family. We had Rudy flown in from Minnesota and picked him up at the airport when he was eight weeks old. We all fell in love with him instantly. He was the cutest little puppy I'd ever seen with his lush white coat. Rudy is now ten and has been with us through it all. I often look at him and marvel at his beauty. I've never loved an animal the way I've loved Rudy. He's been by my side as my steady companion these past three years and I often wonder what he thinks or what he would say if he could speak. I also try to remember where he was the morning Trent passed. I've tried hard to recall if Rudy was in our bedroom when Trent came upstairs to the foot of our bed and collapsed. I can see the EMTs working on Trent and remember screaming and telling them to be careful as they took him downstairs for fear they wouldn't be able to hold him up. I remember running out of the house, but I don't remember where Rudy was. I remember coming back home from the hospital in shock and disbelief that Trent had passed and friends and family pouring in our house throughout the day, but I don't remember Rudy. I don't remember a lot from that day, or the days, weeks and months that followed. But I do remember realizing a few weeks later that Rudy was a different dog. He too was grieving. What I didn't know is that he was also in physical pain and would later be diagnosed with a torn ACL and arthritis. For months I just thought he was just sad, like we were, but he wasn't playing or running around because he was in pain. It would be almost two years before I finally could see out of my haze that Rudy was suffering from more than his grief. He was limping in pain and needed surgery.

The day I picked up Rudy from surgery was a major trigger. The doctor had told me that he would not be able to walk upstairs for three to six weeks and that his new knee would be stronger than his other knee, but that's about it. When I walked in to pick him up from surgery, he looked at me with his eyes as if to say, "How could you let them do this to me?" He cried a cry I'd never heard before. It was a painful, scared cry. As I was trying to hold back tears at the sight and sound of him, the nurse asked me if I had a crate ready for him or a small room to restrain him in since he was not to walk for six weeks. What? No one told me we would need this. I totally lost it and started bawling hysterically. Flashbacks of cleaning out our storage unit and giving things away after Trent died, trying to remember if I kept the crate, feeling physically sick at Rudy's cries of pain, feeling all alone and wishing Trent was there to help me made me completely lose it. I wasn't about to put Rudy in a crate after he'd just had a surgery. I didn't have a room to close him in and I did not want to isolate him like that. After a few minutes of my breakdown, the nurse brought in the doctor who did the surgery to try to calm me down and assure me he would be OK. I was not only upset, but also furious that they hadn't properly prepared me for the care Rudy would need post-surgery. I had borrowed a baby gate to block the stairs, but that's it. I recalled my mantra of one bite at a time. I took a big deep breath, wiped my eyes, and told them I'd have to come back and get him in thirty minutes. I drove straight to Walmart and bought a toddler yard gate, the kind that extends and can block an entire room or close in an area. When I went back to get Rudy, he was still moaning and crying. I picked up my beloved eighty-pound family member, with a cone around his head and a bandage wrapped around his leg, and drove home. Rudy cried the whole way home. I was distraught and had to cancel my clients for the rest of the day. When Sophia got home from school, we both showered our love on him together the rest of the night. We both slept on the couch because we couldn't leave him alone downstairs. We didn't get much sleep and slept in our own beds the next night, heartbroken, as we said goodnight to him downstairs in his gated area. Neither of us slept very well that night either. The next night I couldn't do it. I couldn't leave him downstairs by himself in pain, with him wondering why he couldn't come up and sleep with us as he had done every night before. So for the next seven weeks, I would carry Rudy upstairs each night and then lift him up to carry him downstairs each morning. I thought to myself and posted on my Facebook page: "This is just another reason to work out and stay strong, fit, and healthy. So you can carry your eighty-pound dog up and down the stairs."

Dogs Are Spirits Having a Dog Experience

About a month before the one year anniversary of Trent's passing, I woke up feeling really sad and decided to stay in bed. It was a rainy Saturday and I was by myself. I was tired from a long work week and struggling to face the upcoming anniversary, his birthday, our anniversary, and then the holidays. I hadn't had a good cry in a while and I let myself have it that morning. I must have cried for two straight hours. The ugly kind of cry with moans, lots of snot and tissues, and an outpour of emotions. The entire time, Rudy was right next to me, lying down on his bed. After a couple of hours of my crying, all of the sudden, he rose up, looked across the bed to the empty space next to me where Trent once laid, and walked in front of the bed and around to Trent's side. Something he hadn't done since Trent was gone. He proceeded to look at Trent's pillow and whimper. I knew with everything in me what was happening. He was seeing Trent. I started to catch my crying breath so that I could speak and said, "Rudy, do you see Daddy?" His tail began to wag and thump on the floor. I knew it! I had read that dogs could see spirits and I knew at that moment that Trent was lying next to me and that Rudy was showing me he was there. I felt a comforting and protected sensation and my crying stopped. I felt a sense of peace and laid there for a few moments, no longer sobbing and sad, just in awe and embracing the moment for what I knew it was. I don't recall exactly what I did the rest of that day, but I do know I once again got up out of bed to be somebody and turned my day around, feeling more awakened, inspired, connected, and grateful for Rudy.

When I look back at the first year or so after Trent passed, there were many times when I would be in the kitchen with either the kids or friends and family and Rudy would start whining, looking intently at me, as if he was trying to say something. In all of Rudy's seven years, he had never done that before. I now believe that these were times he would see Trent. Have you ever noticed how big the eyes of a Lab are? Or have you ever looked deeply into your own dog's eyes as they stare back into yours, almost *through* you? Have you ever been sick or in despair and felt the love of your dog as he or she nuzzled up to you to comfort you? Or how excited your dog is each and every time you come home and walk through the door? Or witnessed how forgiving your dog is after being scolded or yelled at for chewing something up? A dog's love is unconditional. Dogs love us no matter what. Rudy has taught me the unconditional, healing love of someone who has been and will be by my side for as long as we both shall live, just like Trent's love. Dogs are spirits having a dog experience, just like we are spirits having a human experience. We're all in this life together, part of the Universe supporting each other along our journeys. So when someone says, "Oh, he's just a dog," I can't help but smile as if knowing what I know bonds us even more.

Bird Shit to Bird Shift

I'd never been a fan of birds. I appreciated them and always loved it when I saw a bright red, beautiful cardinal, especially in the winter amidst the white snowcapped trees. But I resisted birds in general and found myself annoyed when I had to wake up earlier than I wanted to because of birds chirping or when I'd find bird poop on my car, house, or deck furniture. Once when I was a young girl still in elementary school, as I walked the rim of my neighbor's sand box pretending to be a gymnast on a parallel beam, I suddenly felt a glop of liquid on my freshly washed hair. Bird poop landed straight on the top of my head raining on my imaginary gymnast parade. From that day on, I would avoid birds and have no desire to engage with them.

It wasn't until 2000 when I brought Sophia home from the hospital as a newborn baby to find a bird's nest in our front door wreath that I reconsidered the symbolism of birds in our lives. Sophia was born in the spring, which has always been my favorite season of the year. Spring represents renewal and rebirth, and for us Midwesterners, the end of the cold, snowy, winter days. The thought of potential bird droppings that come along with this bird's nest did cross my mind, but I was so taken by the idea that baby birds had come to our front door to welcome us home. New life was blooming around us and it was one of the happiest times of my life. I was transitioning into motherhood and reflecting on what I wanted in life.

Much to my surprise, conceiving did not come easy. After almost two and a half years of trying to get pregnant, a surgery for endometriosis, fertility treatments, and a final HCG shot to my ass, we finally conceived. Other than slight nausea in the first trimester, I had a really easy and good pregnancy. I was so grateful to be pregnant and thought that I was blessed with an easy pregnancy because of all of the difficulty I went through to get pregnant. Although I loved my job as a brand manager and loved working with my boss, who would become a lifelong friend, I yearned for a way to spend more time with Sophia, for fear of missing out as a full-time working mom.

Life would teach me later, that being a working mom offers, among other things, invaluable lessons to your children: the value of doing fulfilling work that you love, self-worth, growth, self-sufficiency, independence and the ability to manage two full-time jobs—motherhood and working outside the home. For many years I would secretly wonder what it would be like to not have to work and wish for just the option to be a stay-at-home mom or work part time. Throughout my corporate career, I would find myself at a work-related coffee or lunch meeting with a client, dressed in my suit and heels, discussing various business topics and glancing at a stay-at-home mom in her yoga pants with her child in tow, wondering what that would feel like. A no pressure outing with no business agenda—I could only dream, I thought. Then the voice would chime in my head to say how lucky I was that I could do work that I enjoyed and be so independent, to earn my own money and take care of myself and my family and be able to do it all. I could have never imagined one day owning my own business, working from home, and getting together for coffee and lunch meetings in my yoga pants and sneakers. It would take a divine life changing force to awaken me and thrust me into this life that I once yearned for.

One day, about two years into my new normal, I was looking out from my kitchen window as I washed dishes. When you eat healthy and cook with real, fresh foods, there tends to be more knives from chopping vegetables; pots and pans from preparing and cooking real foods; and a blender for smoothies that need to be hand-washed on a daily basis. I'd seen a segment on SuperSoul Sunday a couple years ago that changed the way I looked at washing dishes. I no longer approached dish washing as a dreaded task, but as a ritual with gratitude for healthy foods to eat, free flowing warm water at my fingertips, able hands to scrub, dishes to be able to wash, a cozy kitchen to eat in and gather with family and friends, and a peaceful view out my kitchen window. As I thought about these blessings, I saw three birds outside my window making a nest. I said out loud to myself that I needed to embrace birds more as part of my awakening of all things good in the Universe. Since I'd been observing and noticing more about nature in general and my surroundings, I'd been observing and marveling at the flights and songs of birds during my outdoor walks and runs and awaking to birds chirping outside my window. The very next day, my friend and neighbor, Susan, brought me over a gift bag and said she saw this bird and thought I should have it.

Another goose bumps, giddy, aha moment of pure amazement. I had just declared a new appreciation for birds and the consequential shift was immediately supported by the Universe. No more fear of bird poop, just a pure new found love for birds. This shift in thinking transformed my thoughts toward these beautiful winged creatures. They now make me smile when I awake to their morning song. I got the message and reveled in the sweet songs of melodies pure and true. Thank you, Mr. Marley, I finally get your inspirational message.

Rise up this mornin',
Smiled with the risin' sun,
Three little birds,
Pitch by my doorstep
Singin' sweet songs,
Of melodies pure and true,
Sayin', "This is my message to you."
—Bob Marley

CHAPTER 6

Lesson: Serving Others Serves Your Purpose

"The key to your destiny is to remember your dream."

—Joel Osteen

It took me thirteen years to remember my dream and bring it to life. Actually, when I dig deep, the seed was planted much before, back when I was in college at West Virginia University in 1988. When I needed to pick a major the second semester of my sophomore year, I was trying to figure out what I wanted to do and be when I grew up. I knew I was really interested in health and nutrition. My friend Sally was majoring in nutrition; I was completely intrigued with it and got excited about the idea of a career in this field of study. I loved everything about food and healthy eating, so the idea of helping people with their health and nutrition and earning a living from it completely lit me up. It was a dream job for me, except for one thing—the fear that I couldn't pass the math and chemistry classes required for a nutrition degree. My lack of belief in myself held me back. I didn't believe in myself enough to put my ass where my heart was and do the work, so I chose fear instead of love for my dream. I didn't have the courage at the age of nineteen to follow my heart.

I decided I had to find a new dream job, one that didn't require as many math and science classes; one that my right-brained mind could do more easily. Yep, I took the easy way out and scanned the college curriculum for a major that had the least amount of math classes. I chose journalism, with a minor in marketing. I ended up really loving my journalism, public relations, and marketing classes and excelled my junior and senior years of college. I thought I'd lucked out and had found my non-math calling and was very happy. Not only did it naturally make me happy, but I chose to be happy with my decision and it served me well for many years. I believe now that I was meant to take the path I did to lead me to be better equipped and more well-rounded in my education, business sense, and skill set so that I would be ready for this next chapter in my life. What I learned along my journey helped me to be better today at working to serve others in health and fitness. Not only to live it, but to write and share it through communication channels like my website, social media, blogs, my Weekly Wellness Bites™ newsletter, workshops, and this book.

What I know for sure is that it's never too late to follow your heart. And when we set out to serve others, we can be reminded of and awakened to our dreams, our destiny, and our purpose. As one of my favorite ministers and teachers, Joel Osteen, has said, "The key to your destiny is to remember your dream." Years may pass us by as we go through the days, getting by feeling content, yet not completely fulfilled. But we must remember that each of us was born destined for our own personal greatness and with dreams inside us. We often forget about our childhood or young adulthood dreams and aspirations along our journey. Or we may lose sight of our dreams when someone tells us it's not possible, it's too late or that we're not good enough. We may even allow that voice inside our own heads attempting to dim our light by bullying us into questioning who we think we are to think we could achieve our dreams and aspirations. The key really is to do a "gut check", leverage our internal super human power and remember that our dreams were once there inside us. If the dream is in us, it is possible to accomplish it. As Joel says, "We can either talk ourselves into our dreams or we can talk ourselves out of our dreams!" I have talked myself out of my real dreams a few times over the years. Those were make or break moments when I chose fear (of failing or the unknown) instead of love (for my dream, my authentic life, and my faith in myself). Those were years I let fear of failing or worrying about the what-ifs talk me out of following my heart.

    For me, it took a life changing painful event that shattered me and broke me down and open to pursue one of my dreams. I was finally broken open to believing in the possibilities and letting go of fear, for the pain of not doing it became worse than actually finally doing it. I was already in such emotional pain that the pain of not taking that first step—that first bite—was worse than taking it. Remembering my dream and following my heart not only helped heal me, but it brought me back to what I believe is my destiny. To serve others through health and wellness to live their best, healthiest, happiest, most inspired lives.

I've always known that volunteering and acts of service brought me joy and an overall good and happy feeling. But what I've learned during my own transformation and what I know for sure is that when we are serving others, we're not just serving our purpose but service itself serves a greater purpose, and that our passion is what leads us to our purpose.

If you want to discover your purpose (and rediscover your dream), find a way to serve and "practice your dream job or dream life" through a channel that you have an interest in or find something you're already good at and figure out how to share it with others. Identify something you have a passion for or a cause close to your heart, and ask yourself these two simple questions:

1. If money wasn't a concern, how would you explore your passion or curiosity?
2. If you followed your heart, where would it take you?

This is how I coach my clients and teach through my writing and workshops: to help remember your dreams, serve your purpose, and live out your best, healthiest, happiest, most inspired life, start to visualize what that would look and *feel* like. Creative visualization is simply the practice of using your imagination to create what you want in your life; to go from wondering about the what-ifs to *wandering* about the possibilities. As we create what we want in our life, we can manifest our dreams and our purpose.

Creative visualization can be a discovery into what's been holding us back and identifying fears that block us from achieving balance and living out our best, happiest life.

Once we dig deep within to see more clearly, we can eliminate past fears, negative self-talk and limiting beliefs, leaving space for us to discover and manifest our dreams and purpose. And then we can take the next step—next bite—to achieving the life and experiences we yearn for, one bite at a time.

If you're not sure of what you're passionate about, ask yourself the following questions. Remember to think and dream big but also remember to pay close attention to the little things that pop in your mind when you ask yourself:

1. What lights you up and makes you smile? (What activities, people, events, hobbies, projects get you excited, energized, and make you happy when you're doing them?)

2. What did you dream about and what were your favorite things to do when you were younger? What about now?
3. What gets you psyched to get out of bed in the morning or what activities do you look forward to doing when you get home from work or on the weekend?
4. When you were younger—a child, a teenager or freshly starting out in your twenties—who did you want to *be* in life?
5. What makes you feel great about yourself?
6. What do you look forward to doing "one day"? What do you daydream about doing?
7. If you won the lottery, what is something you would want to do but haven't yet because money was holding you back? What would you stop doing and start doing instead?
8. If you were to die tomorrow, what would you regret not doing, being, or having in your life?
9. If you followed your heart, where would it take you?

Start by looking for opportunities to volunteer and help someone else in the areas you found yourself answering to in the questions above. Think of how you can show up and put yourself in environments, new settings, and situations that support your passion or hobby. Surround yourself with like-minded people and reach out to others already in the arena you aspire to be in. Find or create a tribe that supports your vibe. Don't just follow your heart. Put your ass where your heart is and reframe your thinking to believe that whatever dream is inside you, it's possible to achieve it and that it's never too late!

One of my favorite authors who has inspired me ever since I saw him on SuperSoul Sunday talking with Oprah is Mark Nepo. He says, "Happiness is the joy we feel when we're striving toward our potential." His message struck a chord with me because I remember I felt happiness—an emotion I didn't think I would ever feel again after I lost my husband—when I started exercising again to feel better and not cry. And then feeling unexpected and actual joy at the idea of helping others heal, feel, and live better through health and fitness. Those feelings of joy continued to grow as I believed it was possible and strived toward my potential, following my dream and putting my ass where my heart was to start my own business, working to serve others through health and fitness—my new life's work. As the Universe would have it, a few months after I was inspired by Mark's conversation with Oprah, one of my newer clients gave me a copy his book, *The Book of Awakening*, thinking I might like it based on some of the things I was working on with her and using in our coaching sessions. I think in the beginning she wasn't sure how to take some of my coaching methods or out of the traditional training box of thinking and teaching, but I knew even though she was a "just the facts kind of girl" she was curious and seeking more. She has since become a dear friend and as with everyone that God puts in my life, I know Lanae was another Godsend in many ways and that we are here to help each other in our own unique and special ways along our journeys.

Serving my new purpose was my self-prescribed grief therapy and awakened me to the dream that had been inside me for years, leading me to my destiny and continuing the next chapter of my journey. It led me to know for sure that what my fellow Hoosier, Diane Sawyer, said is true: "The dream is not the destiny, but the journey." I understood that learning to embrace the process and the journey creates a transformational shift into awakening to the possibilities; into true healing; following our heart's desire; serving our purpose and growing into who we're meant to be, one bite at a time.

CHAPTER 7

Lesson: Embrace The Process

"Follow Your Heart."

- Unknown, yet said by many

ONE OF THE biggest life lessons I've learned is to embrace the process. Embracing the process isn't just a helpful life coping strategy that allows us to enjoy the journey so much more, it can be life changing in how we flow with, grow from, move through and handle all that life throws at us. Embracing the process is a mindfulness practice and can be learned as part of creating a healthier, happier lifestyle.

When I coach my clients in practicing this habit of mindfully embracing the process, amazing things start to happen. They're able to create the changes they've been wanting and enjoy the journey as a result.

When we're so focused on the desired outcome or end result, we not only miss out on all of the lessons but also on all of the fun! Experiencing the journey and embracing the process truly is the fun part of transformation. Whether it's losing weight and getting healthier, starting a business or making a career change, finding your soul mate and starting a family, accomplishing a goal, or overcoming a challenge, by embracing the process, we embrace the journey of our life experiences and can make lasting change as a result. And when we allow ourselves to create transformational change, spread our wings and fly to a higher place, we can live our best, healthiest, happiest most inspired life.

In one of my *Weekly Wellness Bites*, I wrote about how easy it is to get caught up in the daily grind, going through the motions, working toward the end result, and losing sight of embracing the journey to transformational change. Here is an excerpt from that piece:

> Sometimes when we get stuck in old habits or suffocating patterns, whether it's working too much, not exercising, eating healthy, or getting enough

sleep, or allowing over scheduling and stress to take over, we tell ourselves the story we make up in our heads to justify or rationalize why we aren't spreading our wings and flying into a higher place.

Even though everything in us yearns for more, feels off center, edgy, resentful or completely drained—the mind and body's way of saying we're out of balance—we keep going down the same path, spending time with the same people.

Notice I say going "down" the same path instead of going "Up," as in rising **up** and out of it. As in pausing to get still and wake **UP** to who we were meant to be!

If you've been practicing putting into action anything that I've shared in previous Weekly Wellness Bites—

> **Embracing the Process**
> **Creative Visualization**
> **Making Your To-BE List**
> **Writing Your Younger Self a Love Letter**
> **Closing Your Eyes So You Can See More Clearly**
> **Doing Something That Takes Your Breath Away**
> or
> **Going Where Your Heart Would Take You If You Followed It**

…then you're practicing being more mindful, becoming more aware of your internal power, and if you're taking action, then you are in a state of transformation.

Having been the caterpillar who others thought at first I was weird, crazy or out of my mind to make the changes I've made during my own transformation, I can assure you it's good to be a butterfly! Not just good, it's a beautiful gift to BE your true self, follow your heart, explore your passions and rise up to take a leap of faith. To go UP a different path. **Especially** when they think you're weird and crazy. Because when they do, you're definitely on to something—BIGGER and BETTER!

Know there will most certainly be those people in your circle—caterpillars—who will question you, try to create fear and hold you back because it makes THEM uncomfortable to see you change, awaken to your higher self and transform.

Remember **you've always had the power** and now that you're learning it for yourself, you get to choose how high you spread your wings and fly.

Wherever you are along your journey, embrace the process and know that you are loved and supported and that I am rooting for you, believing in you and part of the Universe that's "got you."

As I began my journey to heal and transform, there were a lot of people who thought I was crazy and had lost my mind. In the past, I would have let other people's judgments create fear and doubt in myself and hold me back. But as a result of being broken down and broken open, one of the shifts that naturally occurred was my pain overruled any past fears and allowed me to spread my wings and fly higher, out of my grief and into my new normal.

The plaque pictured at the front of this chapter which reads "Follow Your Heart" was given to me by a friend and colleague, Jackie, upon my departure at my former company. I was leaving after twelve years to follow my heart and this beautifully crafted artwork reaffirmed my calling. This plaque still sits in my studio reminding me and everyone who enters to follow our hearts and embrace the process.

As I write this, it's been three years and nine months since Trent passed on. I realized I had experienced PTSD (post-traumatic stress syndrome) the first couple of years. I didn't know what it was at the time, but it's clear now that I suffered from PTSD. Recently, I read in Shawn Achor's book, *The Happiness Advantage*—another must read if you haven't heard of it—a new term called *post-traumatic transformation*. This is what happens when we experience a traumatic event and are transformed in a positive and better way. This was a big aha discovery for me. Finally, a phrase that helps identify the silver lining and positive changes that can happen after a trauma! This phase of post-traumatic transformation is the gift we get for going through the darkness and choosing to crawl out, spread our wings, and rise higher—out of the darkness and into the light; out of the traumatic stress syndrome phase and into the transformational growth stage.

Like me, you might know someone who has had cancer say that their cancer made them a better person, or that it was the best thing to ever happen to them. Sounds odd at first, but I get it. Finding my husband was one of the best things that ever happened to me, and losing him ultimately made me a better person. I began my transformation soon after he died without even realizing it. When I chose to be a victor and not a victim, and not allow a second tragedy to occur by honoring my own life by getting up, moving forward and rising higher into my new normal, the transformation automatically occurred. I could feel God and the Universe supporting me as I surrendered, as I still feel today. I became a seeker and let go of any past worries or fears. As Dr. Christiane Northrup teaches, "We must feel it to heal it." I let myself feel all of what I was feeling, even when I was in pure misery and disbelief, and I let the healing begin.

One of the best gifts we can give to ourselves is to honor and embrace the process of life and death, because everything we do matters. Every situation and circumstance we face can transform us to live happier and healthier. When we seek to awaken from times of darkness or even the slightest life challenge, we can begin—as David Harkin's transforming poem sent by my friend Kristy teaches us—"to be happy for tomorrow because of yesterday."

If you're still here on earth, your work is not done and your life as it is today matters. What I've learned and know for sure is that you have the power to change your life and to transform from anything and everything that happens to and *for* you. You can grow from everything that you experience, no matter how difficult. It's never too late to be inspired by that dream inside you; to be inspired by your own life.

Harvard researcher and author Shawn Achor calls this choosing our "positive reality." I love it when science and research supports and proves what the Universe and life is already teaching us. In Shawn's book *Before Happiness* (Remember earlier I recommended you read his first book, *The Happiness Advantage*?), he shares, "It is by experience that we discover and by science that we prove." Everything I've ever experienced about grief, divorce, loss, and how we *choose* to get through other difficult experiences and come out the other side transformed and, yes, happy is proven by science that we do have the power to change and create our own positive reality. To smile and go on, and thus live our best, healthiest, happiest, most inspired lives.

Shawn writes that:

Success on a massive scale requires a reality in which, even if our conscious minds can't see a solution, our unconscious minds know that one is possible. One conclusion has remained constant (in all his research and work around the globe): there is a big difference between being smart and being inspired. To be inspired you need to stop seeing the world through the same old lens. If you can't learn to change your reality, you'll never be truly inspired. Information alone does not cause transformation. The key now is to incorporate just a few strategies, maybe just one at a time (yes, just one bite at a time) into your life.

The benefits of changing your reality—and sharing that positive reality with others—are the kinds of successes, discoveries, and breakthroughs that can transform not only your own life but the world.

Thank you, Shawn, for sharing your breakthrough scientific research that proves we have the power to heal, grow, recover, and transform our lives. The research validates each of the seven life lessons that I share in this book. We *can* change our reality and transform our life, one bite at a time.

Final Thoughts

This isn't the end, it's just the beginning and part of the process. Both yours and mine. For we are all in this life together, connected by our stories. May the insights and lessons shared in this book speak to you and serve you in the way in which you need to own your story and be inspired by your own life. To remember these seven life lessons as a guidepost along your own journey when life knocks you down, hits you by surprise, or changes in an instant, so you can break through, rise up from your suffering and be awakened to the possibilities. To remember that through all suffering - every challenge, hardship or tragedy lies a lesson and an opportunity to grow and be transformed. May you remember to:

1. Take it one bite at a time - remember to take a deep breath, as you ask yourself, "How do you eat an elephant?"
2. Make tough choices for the right reasons - with the right intentions, trusting all will be well, perhaps "even better."

3. Leverage your super human power - get in touch with your internal guide, do a gut check and remember your power is always within you.
4. Show up and keep showing up - for others and yourself throughout suffering, shining and healing with your light and love.
5. Awaken to the magic and love of animals - notice and embrace the presence and beauty of all living beings, remembering the Universe supports you.
6. Follow your heart - then do the work remembering it's never too late.
7. Embrace the process - *choose* to believe you can create your own positive reality and transform your life, having gratitude for the process.

May you rise up to live your best, healthiest, happiest, most inspired life.

One bite at a time.

Acknowledgements

In loving memory of Trent Van Hoosen, my one true eternal love, always and forever.

In honor of my daughter, Sophia, my biggest teacher and inspiration for all that I do.

In honor of my mom, who taught me the love of reading books. I hope this is one we can share together and one that helps you know more about and understand my story.

In honor of my dad, who taught me the value of hard work, resilience, and for always loving and supporting me.

In honor of my brother, John, who by the end of writing this book, taught me the true meaning of forgiveness. Thank you for your loving example and waking me up to what I thought I already knew.

In honor of Matt and Joe, my "bonus" sons and the best gifts your father gave me. May you always know my love for you is unconditional.

Last but not least, I am eternally grateful for my girlfriends and soul sisters who have carried me through it all. God blessed me with the best girlfriends in lieu of sisters. Without you, my story would be very different.

For my teachers whom I have not met, I thank you for sharing your beautiful and inspiring work that taught and guided me through over the years. And special thanks to Oprah Winfrey and the OWN Network for introducing me to many of these authors and teachers, inspiring me to heal, grow, love, remember my dream, and discover my purpose to help others live their best, healthiest, happiest, and most inspired lives.

Here's to you Joel Osteen, Louise Hay, Dr. Wayne Dyer, Deepak Chopra, Marianne Williamson, Gabby Bernstein, Gary Zukav, Jack Canfield, Jack Kornfield, Brene' Brown, Steven Pressfield, Miguel Ruiz, Mark Nepo, Dr. Christiane Northrup, and the countless SuperSoul Sunday teachers who have inspired me with each lesson, book and story you shared.

Inspirational Reading List

Books that have inspired, healed, and transformed me (in alphabetical order):

7 Spiritual Laws of Success, by Deepak Chopra
90 Minutes in Heaven, by Don Piper
A Purpose Driven Life, by Rick Warren
An Awakened Life, by Mark Nepo
Angels Among Us, by Sophia Burnham
Awaken the Spirit Within, by Rebecca Rosen
Before Happiness, by Shawn Achor
Daring Greatly, by Brene' Brown
Do the Work, by Steven Pressfield
Goddesses Never Age, by Dr. Christiane Northrup
Heaven Is for Real by Todd Burpo and Lynn Vincent
Jesus Calling, by Sarah Young
Many Lives, Many Masters, by Brian Weiss
Seat of the Soul, by Gary Zukav
Spirit Junkie, by Gabrielle Bernstein
The 7 Habits of Highly Effective People, by Stephen R. Covey
The Alchemist, by Paul Coelho

The Four Agreements, by Don Miguel Ruiz, specifically the 2nd Agreement
The Happiness Advantage, by Shawn Achor
The Power of Intention, by Dr. Wayne Dyer
Thrive, by Arianna Huffington
The Secret, by Rhonda Byrne
Why People Don't Heal and How They Can, by Caroline Myss
You Can Heal Your Life, by Louise Hay

About the Author

Susan Van Hoosen was forced to re-evaluate her life's purpose after the sudden death of her husband. Trading in her "suits for sneakers," she was inspired by fitness to leave a twenty-year career in marketing and sales and founded Inspired by Fitness, LLC, to serve others through health and wellness. Through her one-bite-at-a-time approach, her mission is to help people live their best, healthiest, happiest, and most-inspired lives.

Susan is a certified health coach, fitness trainer, speaker, author and E-RYT 200 Yoga teacher in training. She lives with her daughter, Sophia, and beloved lab, Rudy, in Fishers, Indiana.

Connect Online and Contact Susan for
Speaking Engagements, Coaching and Workshops
www.susanvanhoosen.com
Twitter @SusanVanHoosen
LinkedIn @ Susan Van Hoosen
Facebook @ Inspired By Fitness

www.ingramcontent.com/pod-product-compliance
Lightning Source LLC
Chambersburg PA
CBHW032303300426
44110CB00033B/449